THE TALES OF CHEKHOV
VOLUME 1

THE DARLING
AND OTHER STORIES

THE TALES OF CHEKHOV

THE DARLING

AND OTHER STORIES

By
ANTON CHEKHOV

Translated By
CONSTANCE GARNETT

The Ecco Press
New York

The Ecco Press logo by Ahmed Yacoubi

Library of Congress Cataloging in Publication Data
Chekhov, Anton Pavlovich, 1860–1904.
The darling and other stories.
(The tales of Chekhov, vol. 1)
Reprint. Originally published: New York: Macmillan, 1917.
Contents: The darling–Tolstoy's criticism on "The darling"–Ariadne–[etc.]
1. Chekhov, Anton Pavlovich, 1860–1904.
Translations, English. I. Title.
II. Series: Chekhov, Anton Pavlovich, 1860–1904.
Short stories. English; v. 1.
PG3456.A15G3   1984   vol. 1   891.73'3s   83-16546
ISBN 0-88001-038-X   [891.73'3]

CONTENTS

THE DARLING

THE DARLING
AND OTHER STORIES

THE DARLING

OLENKA, the daughter of the retired collegiate asses-
sor, Plemyanniakov, was sitting in her back porch,
lost in thought.   It was hot, the flies were persistent
and teasing, and it was pleasant to reflect that it
would soon be evening.   Dark rainclouds were gathering from the east, and bringing from time to time
a breath of moisture in the air.

Kukin, who was the manager of an open-air theatre
called the Tivoli, and who lived in the lodge, was
standing in the middle of the garden looking at the
sky.

" Again! " he observed despairingly.   " It's going to rain again!   Rain every day, as though to
spite me.   I might as well hang myself!   It's ruin!
Fearful losses every day."

He flung up his hands, and went on, addressing
Olenka:

" There! that's the life we lead, Olga Semyonovna.   It's enough to make one cry.   One works
and does one's utmost; one wears oneself out, getting no sleep at night, and racks one's brain what

to do for the best.   And then what happens?   To begin with, one's public is ignorant, boorish.   I give them the very best operetta, a dainty masque, first rate music-hall artists.   But do you suppose that's what they want!   They don't understand anything of that sort.   They want a clown; what they ask for is vulgarity.   And then look at the weather!   Almost every evening it rains.   It started on the tenth of May, and it's kept it up all May and June.   It's simply awful!   The public doesn't come, but I've to pay the rent just the same. and pay the artists."

The next evening the clouds would gather again, and Kukin would say with an hysterical laugh:

" Well, rain away, then!   Flood the garden, drown me!   Damn my luck in this world and the next!   Let the artists have me up!   Send me to prison! — to Siberia! — the   scaffold!   Ha,   ha, ha!"

And next day the same thing.

Olenka listened to Kukin with silent gravity, and sometimes tears came into her eyes.   In the end his misfortunes touched her; she grew to love him. He was a small thin man, with a yellow face, and curls combed forward on his forehead.   He spoke in a thin tenor; as he talked his mouth worked on one side, and there was always an expression of despair on his face; yet he aroused a deep and genuine affection in her.   She was always fond of some one, and could not exist without loving.   In earlier days

she had loved her papa, who now sat in a darkened
room, breathing with difficulty; she had loved her
aunt who used to come every other year from
Bryansk; and before that, when she was at school,
she had loved her French master.   She was a gen-
tle, soft-hearted, compassionate girl, with mild, tender eyes and very good health.   At the sight of her
full rosy cheeks, her soft white neck with a little
dark mole on it, and the kind, naïve smile, which
came into her face when she listened to anything
pleasant, men thought, " Yes, not half bad," and
smiled too, while lady visitors could not refrain from
seizing her hand in the middle of a conversation, ex-
claiming in a gush of delight, " You darling! "

The house in which she had lived from her birth
upwards, and which was left her in her father's
will, was at the extreme end of the town, not far from
the Tivoli.   In the evenings and at night she could
hear the band playing, and the crackling and bang-
ing of fireworks, and it seemed to her that it was
Kukin struggling with his destiny, storming the en-
trenchments of his chief foe, the indifferent public;
there was a sweet thrill at her heart, she had no desire to sleep, and when he returned home at daybreak, she tapped softly at her bedroom window, and
showing him only her face and one shoulder through
the curtain, she gave him a friendly smile. . . .

He proposed to her, and they were married.   And
when he had a closer view of her neck and her plump,
fine shoulders, he threw up his hands, and said:

" You darling! "

He was happy, but as it rained on the day and night of his wedding, his face still retained an expression of despair.

They got on very well together. She used to sit in his office, to look after things in the Tivoli, to put down the accounts and pay the wages. And her rosy cheeks, her sweet, naïve, radiant smile, were to be seen now at the office window, now in the refreshment bar or behind the scenes of the theatre. And already she used to say to her acquaintances that the theatre was the chief and most important thing in life, and that it was only through the drama that one could derive true enjoyment and become cultivated and humane.

" But do you suppose the public understands that? " she used to say. " What they want is a clown. Yesterday we gave ' Faust Inside Out,' and almost all the boxes were empty; but if Vanitchka and I had been producing some vulgar thing, I assure you the theatre would have been packed. To-morrow Vanitchka and I are doing ' Orpheus in Hell.' Do come."

And what Kukin said about the theatre and the actors she repeated. Like him she despised the public for their ignorance and their indifference to art; she took part in the rehearsals, she corrected the actors, she kept an eye on the behaviour of the musicians, and when there was an unfavourable notice in the local paper, she shed tears, and then went to the editor's office to set things right.

The actors were fond of her and used to call her " Vanitchka and I," and " the darling "; she was sorry for them and used to lend them small sums of money, and if they deceived her, she used to shed a few tears in private, but did not complain to her husband.

They got on well in the winter too. They took the theatre in the town for the whole winter, and let it for short terms to a Little Russian company, or to a conjurer, or to a local dramatic society. Olenka grew stouter, and was always beaming with satisfaction, while Kukin grew thinner and yellower, and continually complained of their terrible losses, although he had not done badly all the winter. He used to cough at night, and she used to give him hot raspberry tea or lime-flower water, to rub him with eau-de-Cologne and to wrap him in her warm shawls.

" You're such a sweet pet! " she used to say with perfect sincerity, stroking his hair. " You're such a pretty dear! "

Towards Lent he went to Moscow to collect a new troupe, and without him she could not sleep, but sat all night at her window, looking at the stars, and she compared herself with the hens, who are awake all night and uneasy when the cock is not in the hen-house. Kukin was detained in Moscow, and wrote that he would be back at Easter, adding some instructions about the Tivoli.   But on the Sunday before Easter, late in the evening, came a sudden ominous knock at the gate; some one was hammering on the gate as though on a barrel — boom, boom, boom!   The drowsy cook went flopping with her bare feet through the puddles, as she ran to open the gate.

"Please open," said some one outside in a thick bass.   "There is a telegram for you."

Olenka had received telegrams from her husband before, but this time for some reason she felt numb with terror.   With shaking hands she opened the telegram and read as follows:

"Ivan Petrovitch died suddenly to-day.   Awaiting immate instructions fufuneral Tuesday."

That was how it was written in the telegram — "fufuneral," and the utterly incomprehensible word "immate."   It was signed by the stage manager of the operatic company.

"My darling!" sobbed Olenka.   "Vanitchka, my precious, my darling!   Why did I ever meet you!   Why did I know you and love you!   Your poor heart-broken Olenka is all alone without you!"

Kukin's funeral took place on Tuesday in Moscow, Olenka returned home on Wednesday, and as soon as she got indoors she threw herself on her bed and sobbed so loudly that it could be heard next door, and in the street.

"Poor darling!" the neighbours said, as they

crossed themselves. "Olga Semyonovna, poor darling! How she does take on!"

Three months later Olenka was coming home from mass, melancholy and in deep mourning. It happened that one of her neighbours, Vassily Andreitch Pustovalov, returning home from church, walked back beside her. He was the manager at Babakayev's, the timber merchant's. He wore a straw hat, a white waistcoat, and a gold watch-chain, and looked more like a country gentleman than a man in trade.

"Everything happens as it is ordained, Olga Semyonovna," he said gravely, with a sympathetic note in his voice; "and if any of our dear ones die, it must be because it is the will of God, so we ought to have fortitude and bear it submissively."

After seeing Olenka to her gate, he said good-bye and went on. All day afterwards she heard his sedately dignified voice, and whenever she shut her eyes she saw his dark beard. She liked him very much. And apparently she had made an impression on him too, for not long afterwards an elderly lady, with whom she was only slightly acquainted, came to drink coffee with her, and as soon as she was seated at table began to talk about Pustovalov, saying that he was an excellent man whom one could thoroughly depend upon, and that any girl would be glad to marry him. Three days later Pustovalov came himself. He did not stay long, only about ten minutes, and he did not say much, but when he left, Olenka loved him — loved him so much that she lay awake all night in a perfect fever, and in the morning she sent for the elderly lady. The match was quickly arranged, and then came the wedding.

Pustovalov and Olenka got on very well together when they were married.

Usually he sat in the office till dinner-time, then he went out on business, while Olenka took his place, and sat in the office till evening, making up accounts and booking orders.

"Timber gets dearer every year; the price rises twenty per cent," she would say to her customers and friends.   "Only fancy we used to sell local timber, and now Vassitchka always has to go for wood to the Mogilev district.   And the freight!" she would add, covering her cheeks with her hands in horror. "The freight!"

It seemed to her that she had been in the timber trade for ages and ages, and that the most important and necessary thing in life was timber; and there was something intimate and touching to her in the very sound of words such as "baulk," "post," "beam," "pole," "scantling," "batten," "lath," "plank," etc.

At night when she was asleep she dreamed of perfect mountains of planks and boards, and long strings of wagons, carting timber somewhere far away.   She dreamed that a whole regiment of six-inch beams forty feet high, standing on end, was marching upon the timber-yard; that logs, beams, and boards knocked together with the resounding crash of dry wood, kept falling and getting up again, piling themselves on each other. Olenka cried out in her sleep, and Pustovalov said to her tenderly: " Olenka, what's the matter, darling? Cross yourself! "

Her husband's ideas were hers. If he thought the room was too hot, or that business was slack, she thought the same. Her husband did not care for entertainments, and on holidays he stayed at home. She did likewise.

" You are always at home or in the office," her friends said to her. " You should go to the theatre, darling, or to the circus."

" Vassitchka and I have no time to go to theatres," she would answer sedately. " We have no time for nonsense. What's the use of these theatres? "

On Saturdays Pustovalov and she used to go to the evening service; on holidays to early mass, and they walked side by side with softened faces as they came home from church. There was a pleasant fragrance about them both, and her silk dress rustled agreeably. At home they drank tea, with fancy bread and jams of various kinds, and afterwards they ate pie. Every day at twelve o'clock there was a savoury smell of beet-root soup and of mutton or duck in their yard, and on fast-days of fish, and no one could pass the gate without feeling hungry. In the office the samovar was always boiling, and customers were regaled with tea and cracknels. Once a week the couple went to the baths and returned side by side, both red in the face.

"Yes, we have nothing to complain of, thank God," Olenka used to say to her acquaintances. "I wish every one were as well off as Vassitchka and I."

When Pustovalov went away to buy wood in the Mogilev district, she missed him dreadfully, lay awake and cried. A young veterinary surgeon in the army, called Smirnin, to whom they had let their lodge, used sometimes to come in in the evening. He used to talk to her and play cards with her, and this entertained her in her husband's absence. She was particularly interested in what he told her of his home life. He was married and had a little boy, but was separated from his wife because she had been unfaithful to him, and now he hated her and used to send her forty roubles a month for the maintenance of their son. And hearing of all this, Olenka sighed and shook her head. She was sorry for him.

"Well, God keep you," she used to say to him at parting, as she lighted him down the stairs with a candle. "Thank you for coming to cheer me up, and may the Mother of God give you health."

And she always expressed herself with the same sedateness and dignity, the same reasonableness, in imitation of her husband. As the veterinary surgeon was disappearing behind the door below, she would say:

"You know, Vladimir Platonitch, you'd better

make it up with your wife. You should forgive her for the sake of your son. You may be sure the little fellow understands."

And when Pustovalov came back, she told him in a low voice about the veterinary surgeon and his unhappy home life, and both sighed and shook their heads and talked about the boy, who, no doubt, missed his father, and by some strange connection of ideas, they went up to the holy ikons, bowed to the ground before them and prayed that God would give them children.

And so the Pustovalovs lived for six years quietly and peaceably in love and complete harmony.

But behold! one winter day after drinking hot tea in the office, Vassily Andreitch went out into the yard without his cap on to see about sending off some timber, caught cold and was taken ill. He had the best doctors, but he grew worse and died after four months' illness. And Olenka was a widow once more.

"I've nobody, now you've left me, my darling," she sobbed, after her husband's funeral. "How can I live without you, in wretchedness and misery! Pity me, good people, all alone in the world!"

She went about dressed in black with long "weepers," and gave up wearing hat and gloves for good. She hardly ever went out, except to church, or to her husband's grave, and led the life of a nun. It was not till six months later that she took off the weepers and opened the shutters of the windows.

She was sometimes seen in the mornings, going with her cook to market for provisions, but what went on in her house and how she lived now could only be surmised. People guessed, from seeing her drinking tea in her garden with the veterinary surgeon, who read the newspaper aloud to her, and from the fact that, meeting a lady she knew at the post-office, she said to her:

" There is no proper veterinary inspection in our town, and that's the cause of all sorts of epidemics. One is always hearing of people's getting infection from the milk supply, or catching diseases from horses and cows. The health of domestic animals ought to be as well cared for as the health of human beings."

She repeated the veterinary surgeon's words, and was of the same opinion as he about everything. It was evident that she could not live a year without some attachment, and had found new happiness in the lodge. In any one else this would have been censured, but no one could think ill of Olenka; everything she did was so natural. Neither she nor the veterinary surgeon said anything to other people of the change in their relations, and tried, indeed, to conceal it, but without success, for Olenka could not keep a secret. When he had visitors, men serving in his regiment, and she poured out tea or served the supper, she would begin talking of the cattle plague, of the foot and mouth disease, and of the municipal slaughter-houses. He was dreadfully embarrassed, and when the guests had gone, he would seize her by the hand and hiss angrily:

"I've asked you before not to talk about what you don't understand. When we veterinary surgeons are talking among ourselves, please don't put your word in. It's really annoying."

And she would look at him with astonishment and dismay, and ask him in alarm: "But, Voloditchka, what *am* I to talk about?"

And with tears in her eyes she would embrace him, begging him not to be angry, and they were both happy.

But this happiness did not last long. The veterinary surgeon departed, departed for ever with his regiment, when it was transferred to a distant place — to Siberia, it may be. And Olenka was left alone.

Now she was absolutely alone. Her father had long been dead, and his armchair lay in the attic, covered with dust and lame of one leg. She got thinner and plainer, and when people met her in the street they did not look at her as they used to, and did not smile to her; evidently her best years were over and left behind, and now a new sort of life had begun for her, which did not bear thinking about. In the evening Olenka sat in the porch, and heard the band playing and the fireworks popping in the Tivoli, but now the sound stirred no response. She looked into her yard without interest, thought of nothing, wished for nothing, and afterwards, when night came on she went to bed and dreamed of her empty yard.   She ate and drank as it were unwillingly.

And what was worst of all, she had no opinions of any sort.   She saw the objects about her and understood what she saw, but could not form any opinion about them, and did not know what to talk about.   And how awful it is not to have any opinions!   One sees a bottle, for instance, or the rain, or a peasant driving in his cart, but what the bottle is for, or the rain, or the peasant, and what is the meaning of it, one can't say, and could not even for a thousand roubles.   When she had Kukin, or Pustovalov, or the veterinary surgeon, Olenka could explain everything, and give her opinion about anything you like, but now there was the same emptiness in her brain and in her heart as there was in her yard outside.   And it was as harsh and as bitter as wormwood in the mouth.

Little by little the town grew in all directions. The road became a street, and where the Tivoli and the timber-yard had been, there were new turnings and houses.   How rapidly time passes!   Olenka's house grew dingy, the roof got rusty, the shed sank on one side, and the whole yard was overgrown with docks and stinging-nettles.   Olenka herself had grown plain and elderly; in summer she sat in the porch, and her soul, as before, was empty and dreary and full of bitterness.   In winter she sat at her window and looked at the snow.   When she caught the scent of spring, or heard the chime of the church bells, a sudden rush of memories from the past came over her, there was a tender ache in her heart, and her eyes brimmed over with tears; but this was only for a minute, and then came emptiness again and the sense of the futility of life. The black kitten, Briska, rubbed against her and purred softly, but Olenka was not touched by these feline caresses. That was not what she needed. She wanted a love that would absorb her whole being, her whole soul and reason — that would give her ideas and an object in life, and would warm her old blood. And she would shake the kitten off her skirt and say with vexation:

"Get along; I don't want you!"

And so it was, day after day and year after year, and no joy, and no opinions. Whatever Mavra, the cook, said she accepted.

One hot July day, towards evening, just as the cattle were being driven away, and the whole yard was full of dust, some one suddenly knocked at the gate. Olenka went to open it herself and was dumbfounded when she looked out: she saw Smirnin, the veterinary surgeon, grey-headed, and dressed as a civilian. She suddenly remembered everything. She could not help crying and letting her head fall on his breast without uttering a word, and in the violence of her feeling she did not notice how they both walked into the house and sat down to tea.

"My dear Vladimir Platonitch! What fate has

brought you?" she muttered, trembling with joy.

"I want to settle here for good, Olga Semyon-ovna," he told her.   "I have resigned my post, and have come to settle down and try my luck on my own account.   Besides, it's time for my boy to go to school.   He's a big boy.   I am reconciled with my wife, you know."

"Where is she?" asked Olenka.

"She's at the hotel with the boy, and I'm looking for lodgings."

"Good gracious, my dear soul! Lodgings? Why not have my house?   Why shouldn't that suit you?   Why, my goodness, I wouldn't take any rent!" cried Olenka in a flutter, beginning to cry again.   "You live here, and the lodge will do nicely for me.   Oh dear! how glad I am!"

Next day the roof was painted and the walls were whitewashed, and Olenka, with her arms akimbo, walked about the yard giving directions.   Her face was beaming with her old smile, and she was brisk and alert as though she had waked from a long sleep.   The veterinary's wife arrived — a thin, plain lady, with short hair and a peevish expression. With her was her little Sasha, a boy of ten, small for his age, blue-eyed, chubby, with dimples in his cheeks. And scarcely had the boy walked into the yard when he ran after the cat, and at once there was the sound of his gay, joyous laugh.

"Is that your puss, auntie?" he asked Olenka.

The Darling 19

"When she has little ones, do give us a kitten. Mamma is awfully afraid of mice."

Olenka talked to him, and gave him tea. Her heart warmed and there was a sweet ache in her bosom, as though the boy had been her own child. And when he sat at the table in the evening, going over his lessons, she looked at him with deep tenderness and pity as she murmured to herself:

"You pretty pet! . . . my precious! . . . Such a fair little thing, and so clever."

" 'An island is a piece of land which is entirely surrounded by water,' " he read aloud.

"An island is a piece of land," she repeated, and this was the first opinion to which she gave utterance with positive conviction after so many years of silence and dearth of ideas.

Now she had opinions of her own, and at supper she talked to Sasha's parents, saying how difficult the lessons were at the high schools, but that yet the high-school was better than a commercial one, since with a high-school education all careers were open to one, such as being a doctor or an engineer.

Sasha began going to the high school. His mother departed to Harkov to her sister's and did not return; his father used to go off every day to inspect cattle, and would often be away from home for three days together, and it seemed to Olenka as though Sasha was entirely abandoned, that he was not wanted at home, that he was being starved, and she carried him off to her lodge and gave him a little room there.

And for six months Sasha had lived in the lodge with her. Every morning Olenka came into his bedroom and found him fast asleep, sleeping noiselessly with his hand under his cheek. She was sorry to wake him.

"Sashenka," she would say mournfully, "get up, darling. It's time for school."

He would get up, dress and say his prayers, and then sit down to breakfast, drink three glasses of tea, and eat two large cracknels and half a buttered roll. All this time he was hardly awake and a little ill-humoured in consequence.

"You don't quite know your fable, Sashenka," Olenka would say, looking at him as though he were about to set off on a long journey. "What a lot of trouble I have with you! You must work and do your best, darling, and obey your teachers."

"Oh, do leave me alone!" Sasha would say.

Then he would go down the street to school, a little figure, wearing a big cap and carrying a satchel on his shoulder. Olenka would follow him noiselessly.

"Sashenka!" she would call after him, and she would pop into his hand a date or a caramel. When he reached the street where the school was, he would feel ashamed of being followed by a tall, stout woman; he would turn round and say:

"You'd better go home, auntie. I can go the rest of the way alone."

She would stand still and look after him fixedly till he had disappeared at the school-gate.

Ah, how she loved him! Of her former attachments not one had been so deep; never had her soul surrendered to any feeling so spontaneously, so disinterestedly, and so joyously as now that her maternal instincts were aroused. For this little boy with the dimple in his cheek and the big school cap, she would have given her whole life, she would have given it with joy and tears of tenderness. Why? Who can tell why?

When she had seen the last of Sasha, she returned home, contented and serene, brimming over with love; her face, which had grown younger during the last six months, smiled and beamed; people meeting her looked at her with pleasure.

" Good-morning, Olga Semyonovna, darling. How are you, darling? "

" The lessons at the high school are very difficult now," she would relate at the market. " It's too much; in the first class yesterday they gave him a fable to learn by heart, and a Latin translation and a problem. You know it's too much for a little chap."

And she would begin talking about the teachers, the lessons, and the school books, saying just what Sasha said.

At three o'clock they had dinner together: in the evening they learned their lessons together and cried. When she put him to bed, she would stay a long time making the Cross over him and murmuring a prayer;

then she would go to bed and dream of that far-away misty future when Sasha would finish his studies and become a doctor or an engineer, would have a big house of his own with horses and a carriage, would get married and have children. . . . She would fall asleep still thinking of the same thing, and tears would run down her cheeks from her closed eyes, while the black cat lay purring beside her: " Mrr, mrr, mrr."

Suddenly there would come a loud knock at the gate.

Olenka would wake up breathless with alarm, her heart throbbing. Half a minute later would come another knock.

" It must be a telegram from Harkov," she would think, beginning to tremble from head to foot. " Sasha's mother is sending for him from Harkov. . . . Oh, mercy on us ! "

She was in despair. Her head, her hands, and her feet would turn chill, and she would feel that she was the most unhappy woman in the world. But another minute would pass, voices would be heard: it would turn out to be the veterinary surgeon coming home from the club.

" Well, thank God ! " she would think.

And gradually the load in her heart would pass off, and she would feel at ease. She would go back to bed thinking of Sasha, who lay sound asleep in the next room, sometimes crying out in his sleep:

" I'll give it you ! Get away ! Shut up ! "

1899

TOLSTOY'S CRITICISM ON
" THE DARLING "

(From "Readings for Every Day in the Year.")

THERE is a story of profound meaning in the Book
of Numbers which tells how Balak, the King of
the Moabites, sent for the prophet Balaam to curse
the Israelites who were on his borders.   Balak promised Balaam many gifts for this service, and Balaam,
tempted, went to Balak, and went with him up the
mountain, where an altar was prepared with calves
and sheep sacrificed in readiness for the curse.
Balak waited for the curse, but instead of cursing,
Balaam blessed the people of Israel.

Ch. xxiii., v. 11 :   " And Balak said unto Balaam,
What hast thou done unto me?   I took thee to
curse mine enemies, and, behold, thou hast blessed
them altogether.

" 12. And he answered and said, Must I not take
heed to speak that which the Lord hath put in my
mouth?

" 13. And Balak said unto him, Come, I pray
thee, with me into another place . . . and curse
me them from thence."

But again, instead of cursing, Balaam blessed.
And so it was the third time also.

Ch. xxiv., v. 10: "And Balak's anger was kindled against Balaam, and he smote his hands together: and Balak said unto Balaam, I called thee to curse my enemies, and, behold, thou hast altogether blessed them these three times.

"11. Therefore now flee thee to thy place: I thought to promote thee unto great honour; but, lo, the Lord hast kept thee back from honour."

And so Balaam departed without having received the gifts, because, instead of cursing, he had blessed the enemies of Balak.

What happened to Balaam often happens to real poets and artists. Tempted by Balak's gifts, popularity, or by false preconceived ideas, the poet does not see the angel barring his way, though the ass sees him, and he means to curse, and yet, behold, he blesses.

This is just what happened to the true poet and artist Chekhov when he wrote this charming story "The Darling."

The author evidently means to mock at the pitiful creature — as he judges her with his intellect, but not with his heart — the Darling, who after first sharing Kukin's anxiety about his theatre, then throwing herself into the interests of the timber trade, then under the influence of the veterinary surgeon regarding the campaign against the foot and mouth disease as the most important matter in the world, is finally engrossed in the grammatical questions and the interests of the little schoolboy in the big cap.   Kukin's surname is absurd, even his illness and the telegram announcing his death, the timber merchant with his respectability, the veterinary surgeon, even the boy — all are absurd, but the soul of The Darling, with her faculty of devoting herself with her whole being to any one she loves, is not absurd, but marvellous and holy.

I believe that while he was writing " The Darling," the author had in his mind, though not in his heart, a vague image of a new woman; of her equality with man; of a woman mentally developed, learned, working independently for the good of society as well as, if not better than, a man; of the woman who has raised and upholds the woman question; and in writing " The Darling " he wanted to show what woman ought not to be. The Balak of public opinion bade Chekhov curse the weak, submissive undeveloped woman devoted to man; and Chekhov went up the mountain, and the calves and sheep were laid upon the altar, but when he began to speak, the poet blessed what he had come to curse. In spite of its exquisite gay humour, I at least cannot read without tears some passages of this wonderful story.   I am touched by the description of her complete devotion and love for Kukin and all that he cares for, and for the timber merchant and for the veterinary surgeon, and even more of her sufferings when she is left alone and has no one to love; and finally the account of how with all the strength of womanly, motherly feelings (of which she has no experience in her own life) she devotes herself with boundless love to the future man. the schoolboy in the big cap.

The author makes her love the absurd Kukin, the insignificant timber merchant, and the unpleasant veterinary surgeon, but love is no less sacred whether its object is a Kukin or a Spinoza, a Pascal, or a Schiller, and whether the objects of it change as rapidly as with the Darling, or whether the object of it remains the same throughout the whole life.

Some time ago I happened to read in the *Novoe Vremya* an excellent article upon woman. The author has in this article expressed a remarkably clever and profound idea about woman. " Women," he says, " are trying to show us they can do everything we men can do. I don't contest it; I am prepared to admit that women can do everything men can do, and possibly better than men; but the trouble is that men cannot do anything faintly approaching to what women can do."

Yes, that is undoubtedly true, and it is true not only with regard to birth, nurture, and early education of children. Men cannot do that highest, best work which brings man nearest to God — the work of love, of complete devotion to the loved object, which good women have done, do, and will do so well and so naturally. What would become of the world, what would become of us men if women had not that faculty and did not exercise it? We could get on without women doctors, women telegraph clerks, women lawyers, women scientists, women writers, but life would be a sorry affair without mothers, helpers, friends, comforters, who love in men the best in them, and imperceptibly instil, evoke, and support it. There would have been no Magdalen with Christ, no Claire with St. Francis; there would have been no wives of the Dekabrists in Siberia; there would not have been among the Duhobors those wives who, instead of holding their husbands back, supported them in their martyrdom for truth; there would not have been those thousands and thousands of unknown women — the best of all, as the unknown always are — the comforters of the drunken, the weak, and the dissolute, who, more than any, need the comfort of love. That love, whether devoted to a Kukin or to Christ, is the chief, grand, unique strength of woman.

What an amazing misunderstanding it is — all this so-called woman question, which, as every vulgar idea is bound to do, has taken possession of the majority of women, and even of men.

"Woman longs to improve herself"— what can be more legitimate and just than that?

But a woman's work is from her very vocation different from man's, and so the ideal of feminine perfection cannot be the same as the ideal of masculine perfection. Let us admit that we do not know what that ideal is; it is quite certain in any case that it is not the ideal of masculine perfection. And yet it is to the attainment of that masculine ideal that the whole of the absurd and evil activity of the fashionable woman movement, which is such a stumbling-block to woman, is directed.

I am afraid that Chekhov was under the influence of that misunderstanding when he wrote " The Darling."

He, like Balaam, intended to curse, but the god of poetry forbade him, and commanded him to bless. And he did bless, and unconsciously clothed this sweet creature in such an exquisite radiance that she will always remain a type of what a woman can be in order to be happy herself, and to make the happiness of those with whom destiny throws her.

What makes the story so excellent is that the effect is unintentional.

I learnt to ride a bicycle in a hall large enough to drill a division of soldiers.   At the other end of the hall a lady was learning.   I thought I must be careful to avoid getting into her way, and began looking at her.   And as I looked at her I began unconsciously getting nearer and nearer to her, and in spite of the fact that, noticing the danger, she hastened to retreat, I rode down upon her and knocked her down — that is, I did the very opposite of what I wanted to do, simply because I concentrated my attention upon her.

The same thing has happened to Chekhov, but in an inverse sense: he wanted to knock the Darling down, and concentrating upon her the close attention of the poet, he raised her up.

ARIADNE

ARIADNE

ON the deck of a steamer sailing from Odessa to Sevastopol, a rather good-looking gentleman, with a little round beard, came up to me to smoke, and said:

" Notice those Germans sitting near the shelter? Whenever Germans or Englishmen get together, they talk about the crops, the price of wool, or their personal affairs. But for some reason or other when we Russians get together we never discuss anything but women and abstract subjects — but especially women."

This gentleman's face was familiar to me already. We had returned from abroad the evening before in the same train, and at Volotchisk when the luggage was being examined by the Customs, I saw him standing with a lady, his travelling companion, before a perfect mountain of trunks and baskets filled with ladies' clothes, and I noticed how embarrassed and downcast he was when he had to pay duty on some piece of silk frippery, and his companion protested and threatened to make a complaint. Afterwards, on the way to Odessa, I saw him carrying little pies and oranges to the ladies' compartment.

It was rather damp; the vessel swayed a little, and the ladies had retired to their cabins.

The gentleman with the little round beard sat down beside me and continued:

" Yes, when Russians come together they discuss nothing but abstract subjects and women. We are so intellectual, so solemn, that we utter nothing but truths and can discuss only questions of a lofty order. The Russian actor does not know how to be funny; he acts with profundity even in a farce. We're just the same: when we have got to talk of trifles we treat them only from an exalted point of view. It comes from a lack of boldness, sincerity, and simplicity. We talk so often about women, I fancy, because we are dissatisfied. We take too ideal a view of women, and make demands out of all proportion with what reality can give us; we get something utterly different from what we want, and the result is dissatisfaction, shattered hopes, and inward suffering, and if any one is suffering, he's bound to talk of it. It does not bore you to go on with this conversation? "

" No, not in the least."

" In that case, allow me to introduce myself," said my companion, rising from his seat a little: " Ivan Ilyitch Shamohin, a Moscow landowner of a sort. . . . You I know very well."

He sat down and went on, looking at me with a genuine and friendly expression:

" A mediocre philosopher, like Max Nordau, would explain these incessant conversations about women as a form of erotic madness, or would put

it down to our having been slave-owners and so on;
I take quite a different view of it. I repeat, we
are dissatisfied because we are idealists. We want
the creatures who bear us and our children to be
superior to us and to everything in the world. When
we are young we adore and poeticize those with
whom we are in love: love and happiness with us
are synonyms. Among us in Russia marriage without love it despised, sensuality is ridiculed and in-
spires repulsion, and the greatest success is enjoyed
by those tales and novels in which women are beautiful, poetical, and exalted; and if the Russian has
been for years in ecstasies over Raphael's Madonna,
or is eager for the emancipation of women, I assure
you there is no affectation about it. But the trouble
is that when we have been married or been intimate
with a woman for some two or three years, we begin to feel deceived and disillusioned: we pair off
with others, and again — disappointment, again —
repulsion, and in the long run we become convinced
that women are lying, trivial, fussy, unfair, undeveloped, cruel — in fact, far from being superior, are
immeasurably inferior to us men. And in our dissatisfaction and disappointment there is nothing left
for us but to grumble and talk about what we've
been so cruelly deceived in."

While Shamohin was talking I noticed that the
Russian language and our Russian surroundings gave
him great pleasure. This was probably because he
had been very homesick abroad. Though he praised

the Russians and ascribed to them a rare idealism, he did not disparage foreigners, and that I put down to his credit.   It could be seen, too, that there was some uneasiness in his soul, that he wanted to talk more of himself than of women, and that I was in for a long story in the nature of a confession.   And when we had asked for a bottle of wine and had each of us drunk a glass, this was how he did in fact begin:

"I remember in a novel of Weltmann's some one says, ' So that's the story!' and some one else answers, 'No, that's not the story — that's only the introduction to the story.'   In the same way what I've said so far is only the introduction; what I really want to tell you is my own love story.   Excuse me, I must ask you again; it won't bore you to listen?"

I told him it would not, and he went on:

The scene of my story is laid in the Moscow province in one of its northern districts.   The scenery there, I must tell you, is exquisite.   Our homestead is on the high bank of a rapid stream, where the water chatters noisily day and night: imagine a big old garden, neat flower-beds, beehives, a kitchen-garden, and below it a river with leafy willows, which, when there is a heavy dew on them, have a lustreless look as though they had turned grey; and on the other side a meadow, and beyond the meadow on the upland a terrible, dark pine forest.   In that

forest delicious, reddish agarics grow in endless profusion, and elks still live in its deepest recesses.
When I am nailed up in my coffin I believe I shall
still dream of those early mornings, you know, when
the sun hurts your eyes: or the wonderful spring
evenings when the nightingales and the landrails call
in the garden and beyond the garden, and sounds of
the harmonica float across from the village, while
they play the piano indoors and the stream babbles
. . . when there is such music, in fact, that one
wants at the same time to cry and to sing aloud.

We have not much arable land, but our pasture
makes up for it, and with the forest yields about
two thousand roubles a year. I am the only son
of my father; we are both modest persons, and with
my father's pension that sum was amply sufficient
for us.

The first three years after finishing at the university I spent in the country, looking after the estate
and constantly expecting to be elected on some local
assembly; but what was most important, I was violently in love with an extraordinarily beautiful and
fascinating girl. She was the sister of our neighbour, Kotlovitch, a ruined landowner who had on
his estate pine-apples, marvellous peaches, lightning
conductors, a fountain in the courtyard, and at the
same time not a farthing in his pocket. He did
nothing and knew how to do nothing. He was as
flabby as though he had been made of boiled turnip;
he used to doctor the peasants by homœopathy and

was interested in spiritualism. He was, however, a man of great delicacy and mildness, and by no means a fool, but I have no fondness for these gentlemen who converse with spirits and cure peasant women by magnetism. In the first place, the ideas of people who are not intellectually free are always in a muddle, and it's extremely difficult to talk to them; and, secondly, they usually love no one, and have nothing to do with women, and their mysticism has an unpleasant effect on sensitive people. I did not care for his appearance either. He was tall, stout, white-skinned, with a little head, little shining eyes, and chubby white fingers. He did not shake hands, but kneaded one's hands in his. And he was always apologising. If he asked for anything it was " Excuse me "; if he gave you anything it was " Excuse me " too.

As for his sister, she was a character out of a different opera. I must explain that I had not been acquainted with the Kotlovitches in my childhood and early youth, for my father had been a professor at N., and we had for many years lived away. When I did make their acquaintance the girl was twenty-two, had left school long before, and had spent two or three years in Moscow with a wealthy aunt who brought her out into society. When I was introduced and first had to talk to her, what struck me most of all was her rare and beautiful name — Ariadne. It suited her so wonderfully! She was a brunette, very thin, very slender, supple, elegant, and extremely graceful, with refined and exceedingly noble features. Her eyes were shining, too, but her brother's shone with a cold sweetness, mawkish as sugar-candy, while hers had the glow of youth, proud and beautiful. She conquered me on the first day of our acquaintance, and indeed it was inevitable. My first impression was so overwhelming that to this day I cannot get rid of my illusions; I am still tempted to imagine that nature had some grand, marvellous design when she created that girl.

Ariadne's voice, her walk, her hat, even her footprints on the sandy bank where she used to angle for gudgeon, filled me with delight and a passionate hunger for life. I judged of her spiritual being from her lovely face and lovely figure, and every word, every smile of Ariadne's bewitched me, conquered me and forced me to believe in the loftiness of her soul. She was friendly, ready to talk, gay and simple in her manners. She had a poetic belief in God, made poetic reflections about death, and there was such a wealth of varying shades in her spiritual organisation that even her faults seemed in her to carry with them peculiar, charming qualities. Suppose she wanted a new horse and had no money — what did that matter? Something might be sold or pawned, or if the steward swore that nothing could possibly be sold or pawned, the iron roofs might be torn off the lodges and taken to the factory, or at the very busiest time the farm-horses might be driven to the market and sold there for next to nothing. These unbridled desires reduced the whole household to despair at times, but she expressed them with such refinement that everything was forgiven her; all things were permitted her as to a goddess or to Cæsar's wife. My love was pathetic and was soon noticed by every one — my father, the neighbours, and the peasants — and they all sympathised with me. When I stood the workmen vodka, they would bow and say: "May the Kotlovitch young lady be your bride, please God!"

And Ariadne herself knew that I loved her. She would often ride over on horseback or drive in the char-à-banc to see us, and would spend whole days with me and my father. She made great friends with the old man, and he even taught her to bicycle, which was his favourite amusement.

I remember helping her to get on the bicycle one evening, and she looked so lovely that I felt as though I were burning my hands when I touched her. I shuddered with rapture, and when the two of them, my old father and she, both looking so handsome and elegant, bicycled side by side along the main road, a black horse ridden by the steward dashed aside on meeting them, and it seemed to me that it dashed aside because it too was overcome by her beauty. My love, my worship, touched Ariadne and softened her; she had a passionate longing to be captivated like me and to respond with the same love. It was so poetical!

But she was incapable of really loving as I did,

for she was cold and already somewhat corrupted. There was a demon in her, whispering to her day and night that she was enchanting, adorable; and, having no definite idea for what object she was created, or for what purpose life had been given her, she never pictured herself in the future except as very wealthy and distinguished; she had visions of balls, races, liveries, of sumptuous drawing-rooms, of a salon of her own, and of a perfect swarm of counts, princes, ambassadors, celebrated painters and artists, all of them adoring her and in ecstasies over her beauty and her dresses. . . .

This thirst for personal success, and this continual concentration of the mind in one direction, makes people cold, and Ariadne was cold — to me, to nature, and to music. Meanwhile time was passing, and still there were no ambassadors on the scene. Ariadne went on living with her brother, the spiritualist: things went from bad to worse, so that she had nothing to buy hats and dresses with, and had to resort to all sorts of tricks and dodges to conceal her poverty.

As luck would have it, a certain Prince Maktuev, a wealthy man but an utterly insignificant person, had paid his addresses to her when she was living at her aunt's in Moscow. She had refused him, point-blank. But now she was fretted by the worm of repentance that she had refused him; just as a peasant pouts with repulsion at a mug of kvass with cockroaches in it but yet drinks it, so she frowned disdainfully at the recollection of the prince, and yet she would say to me: "Say what you like, there is something inexplicable, fascinating, in a title. . . ."

She dreamed of a title, of a brilliant position, and at the same time she did not want to let me go. However one may dream of ambassadors one's heart is not a stone, and one has wistful feelings for one's youth. Ariadne tried to fall in love, made a show of being in love, and even swore that she loved me. But I am a highly strung and sensitive man; when I am loved I feel it even at a distance, without vows and assurances; at once I felt as it were a coldness in the air, and when she talked to me of love, it seemed to me as though I were listening to the singing of a metal nightingale. Ariadne was herself aware that she was lacking in something. She was vexed and more than once I saw her cry. Another time — can you imagine it? — all of a sudden she embraced me and kissed me. It happened in the evening on the river-bank, and I saw by her eyes that she did not love me, but was embracing me from curiosity, to test herself and to see what came of it. And I felt dreadful. I took her hands and said to her in despair: "These caresses without love cause me suffering!"

"What a queer fellow you are!" she said with annoyance, and walked away.

Another year or two might have passed, and in all probability I should have married her, and so

my story would have ended, but fate was pleased
to arrange our romance differently. It happened
that a new personage appeared on our horizon.
Ariadne's brother had a visit from an old university
friend called Mihail Ivanitch Lubkov, a charming
man of whom coachmen and footmen used to say:
" An entertaining gentleman." He was a man of
medium height, lean and bald, with a face like a
good-natured bourgeois, not interesting, but pale
and presentable, with a stiff, well-kept moustache,
with a neck like gooseskin, and a big Adam's apple.
He used to wear pince-nez on a wide black ribbon,
lisped, and could not pronounce either *r* or *l*. He
was always in good spirits, everything amused
him.

He had made an exceedingly foolish marriage
at twenty, and had acquired two houses in Moscow
as part of his wife's dowry. He began doing them
up and building a bath-house, and was completely
ruined. Now his wife and four children lodged in
Oriental Buildings in great poverty, and he had to
support them — and this amused him. He was thir-
ty-six and his wife was by now forty-two, and that,
too, amused him. His mother, a conceited, sulky
personage, with aristocratic pretensions, despised his
wife and lived apart with a perfect menagerie of
cats and dogs, and he had to allow her seventy-five
roubles a month also; he was, too, a man of taste,
liked lunching at the Slavyansky Bazaar and dining
at the Hermitage; he needed a great deal of money,

but his uncle only allowed him two thousand roubles
a year, which was not enough, and for days together
he would run about Moscow with his tongue out, as
the saying is, looking for some one to borrow from
— and this, too, amused him.   He had come to Kotlovitch to find in the lap of nature, as he said, a rest
from family life.   At dinner, at supper, and on our
walks, he talked about his wife, about his mother,
about his creditors, about the bailiffs, and laughed
at them; he laughed at himself and assured us that,
thanks to his talent for borrowing, he had made
a great number of agreeable acquaintances.   He
laughed without ceasing and we laughed too.   Moreover, in his company we spent our time differently.
I was more inclined to quiet, so to say idyllic pleas-
ures; I liked fishing, evening walks, gathering mushrooms; Lubkov preferred picnics, fireworks, hunt-
ing.   He used to get up picnics three times a week,
and Ariadne, with an earnest and inspired face, used
to write a list of oysters, champagne, sweets, and
used to send me into Moscow to get them, without
inquiring, of course, whether I had money.   And at
the picnics there were toasts and laughter, and again
mirthful descriptions of how old his wife was, what
fat lap-dogs his mother had, and what charming people his creditors were. . . .

Lubkov was fond of nature, but he regarded it
as something long familiar and at the same time,
in reality, infinitely beneath himself and created for
his pleasure.   He would sometimes stand still be-

fore some magnificent landscape and say: "It would be nice to have tea here."

One day, seeing Ariadne walking in the distance with a parasol, he nodded towards her and said:

"She's thin, and that's what I like; I don't like fat women."

This made me wince. I asked him not to speak like that about women before me. He looked at me in surprise and said:

"What is there amiss in my liking thin women and not caring for fat ones?"

I made no answer. Afterwards, being in very good spirits and a trifle elevated, he said:

"I've noticed Ariadne Grigoryevna likes you. I can't understand why you don't go in and win."

His words made me feel uncomfortable, and with some embarrassment I told him how I looked at love and women.

"I don't know," he sighed; "to my thinking, a woman's a woman and a man's a man. Ariadne Grigoryevna may be poetical and exalted, as you say, but it doesn't follow that she must be superior to the laws of nature. You see for yourself that she has reached the age when she must have a husband or a lover. I respect women as much as you do, but I don't think certain relations exclude poetry. Poetry's one thing and love is another. It's just the same as it is in farming. The beauty of nature is one thing and the income from your forests or fields is quite another."

When Ariadne and I were fishing, Lubkov would lie on the sand close by and make fun of me, or lecture me on the conduct of life.

" I wonder, my dear sir, how you can live without a love affair," he would say. " You are young, handsome, interesting — in fact, you're a man not to be sniffed at, yet you live like a monk. Och! I can't stand these fellows who are old at twenty-eight! I'm nearly ten years older than you are, and yet which of us is the younger? Ariadne Grigory-evna, which? "

" You, of course," Ariadne answered him.

And when he was bored with our silence and the attention with which we stared at our floats he went home, and she said, looking at me angrily:

" You're really not a man, but a mush, God forgive me! A man ought to be able to be carried away by his feelings, he ought to be able to be mad, to make mistakes, to suffer! A woman will forgive you audacity and insolence, but she will never forgive your reasonableness! "

She was angry in earnest, and went on:

" To succeed, a man must be resolute and bold. Lubkov is not so handsome as you are, but he is more interesting. He will always succeed with women because he's not like you; he's a man. . . ."

And there was actually a note of exasperation in her voice.

One day at supper she began saying, not address-ing, me that if she were a man she would not stag-

nate in the country, but would travel, would spend
the winter somewhere aboard — in Italy, for instance. Oh, Italy! At this point my father unconsciously poured oil on the flames; he began telling
us at length about Italy, how splendid it was there,
the exquisite scenery, the museums. Ariadne suddenly conceived a burning desire to go to Italy. She
positively brought her fist down on the table and
her eyes flashed as she said: "I must go!"

After that came conversations every day about
Italy: how splendid it would be in Italy — ah, Italy!
— oh, Italy! And when Ariadne looked at me over
her shoulder, from her cold and obstinate expression I saw that in her dreams she had already conquered Italy with all its salons, celebrated foreigners
and tourists, and there was no holding her back now.
I advised her to wait a little, to put off her tour for
a year or two, but she frowned disdainfully and said:
"You're as prudent as an old woman!"

Lubkov was in favour of the tour. He said it
could be done very cheaply, and he, too, would go
to Italy and have a rest there from family life.

I behaved, I confess, as naïvely as a schoolboy.
Not from jealousy, but from a foreboding of something terrible and extraordinary, I tried as far as
possible not to leave them alone together, and they
made fun of me. For instance, when I went in they
would pretend they had just been kissing one another, and so on.

But lo and behold, one fine morning, her plump,

white-skinned brother, the spiritualist, made his appearance and expressed his desire to speak to me alone.

He was a man without will; in spite of his education and his delicacy he could never resist reading another person's letter, if it lay before him on the table.   And now he admitted that he had by chance read a letter of Lubkov's to Ariadne.

" From that letter I learned that she is very shortly going abroad.   My dear fellow, I am very much upset!   Explain it to me for goodness' sake. I can make nothing of it!"

As he said this he breathed hard, breathing straight in my face and smelling of boiled beef.

" Excuse me for revealing the secret of this letter to you, but you are Ariadne's friend, she respects you.   Perhaps you know something of it.   She wants to go away, but with whom?   Mr. Lubkov is proposing to go with her.   Excuse me, but this is very strange of Mr. Lubkov; he is a married man, he has children, and yet he is making a declaration of love; he is writing to Ariadne ' darling.'   Excuse me, but it is so strange!"

I turned cold all over; my hands and feet went numb and I felt an ache in my chest, as if a three-cornered stone had been driven into it.   Kotlovitch sank helplessly into an easy-chair, and his hands fell limply at his sides.

" What can I do?" I inquired.

" Persuade her. . . . Impress her mind. . . .

Just consider, what is Lubkov to her? Is he a match for her? Oh, good God! How awful it is, how awful it is!" he went on, clutching his head. "She has had such splendid offers — Prince Maktuev and . . . and others. The prince adores her, and only last Wednesday week his late grandfather, Ilarion, declared positively that Ariadne would be his wife — positively! His grandfather Ilarion is dead, but he is a wonderfully intelligent person; we call up his spirit every day."

After this conversation I lay awake all night and thought of shooting myself. In the morning I wrote five letters and tore them all up. Then I sobbed in the barn. Then I took a sum of money from my father and set off for the Caucasus without saying good-bye.

Of course, a woman's a woman and a man's a man, but can all that be as simple in our day as it was before the Flood, and can it be that I, a culti- vated man endowed with a complex spiritual organ- isation, ought to explain the intense attraction I feel towards a woman simply by the fact that her bodily formation is different from mine? Oh, how awful that would be! I want to believe that in his strug- gle with nature the genius of man has struggled with physical love too, as with an enemy, and that, if he has not conquered it, he has at least succeeded in tangling it in a net-work of illusions of brother- hood and love; and for me, at any rate, it is no longer a simple instinct of my animal nature as with a dog or a toad, but is real love, and every embrace is spiritualised by a pure impulse of the heart and respect for the woman.   In reality, a disgust for the animal instinct has been trained for ages in hundreds of generations; it is inherited by me in my blood and forms part of my nature, and if I poetize love, is not that as natural and inevitable in our day as my ears' not being able to move and my not being covered with fur?   I fancy that's how the majority of civilised people look at it, so that the absence of the moral, poetical element in love is treated in these days as a phenomenon, as a sign of atavism; they say it is a symptom of degeneracy, of many forms of insanity.   It is true that, in poetizing love, we assume in those we love qualities that are lacking in them, and that is a source of continual mistakes and continual miseries for us.   But to my thinking it is better, even so; that is, it is better to suffer than to find complacency on the basis of woman being woman and man being man.

In Tiflis I received a letter from my father.   He wrote that Ariadne Grigoryevna had on such a day gone abroad, intending to spend the whole winter away.   A month later I returned home.   It was by now autumn.   Every week Ariadne sent my father extremely interesting letters on scented paper, written in an excellent literary style.   It is my opinion that every woman can be a writer.   Ariadne described in great detail how it had not been easy for her to make it up with her aunt and induce the latter to give her a thousand roubles for the journey, and what a long time she had spent in Moscow trying to find an old lady, a distant relation, in order to persuade her to go with her. Such a profusion of detail suggested fiction, and I realised, of course, that she had no chaperon with her.

Soon afterwards I, too, had a letter from her, also scented and literary. She wrote that she had missed me, missed my beautiful, intelligent, loving eyes. She reproached me affectionately for wasting my youth, for stagnating in the country when I might, like her, be living in paradise under the palms, breathing the fragrance of the orange-trees. And she signed herself " Your forsaken Ariadne." Two days later came another letter in the same style, signed " Your forgotten Ariadne." My mind was confused. I loved her passionately, I dreamed of her every night, and then this " your forsaken," " your forgotten "— what did it mean? What was it for? And then the dreariness of the country, the long evenings, the disquieting thoughts of Lubkov. . . . The uncertainty tortured me, and poisoned my days and nights; it became unendurable. I could not bear it and went abroad.

Ariadne summoned me to Abbazzia. I arrived there on a bright warm day after rain; the rain-drops were still hanging on the trees and glistening on the huge, barrack-like *dépendance* where Ariadne and Lubkov were living.

They were not at home. I went into the park;

wandered about the avenues, then sat down. An Austrian General, with his hands behind him, walked past me, with red stripes on his trousers such as our generals wear. A baby was wheeled by in a perambulator and the wheels squeaked on the damp sand. A decrepit old man with jaundice passed, then a crowd of Englishwomen, a Catholic priest, then the Austrian General again. A military band, only just arrived from Fiume, with glittering brass instruments, sauntered by to the bandstand — they began playing.

Have you ever been at Abbazzia? It's a filthy little Slav town with only one street, which stinks, and in which one can't walk after rain without goloshes. I had read so much and always with such intense feeling about this earthly paradise that when afterwards, holding up my trousers, I cautiously crossed the narrow street, and in my ennui bought some hard pears from an old peasant woman who, recognising me as a Russian, said: " Tcheeteery " for " tchetyry " (four) —" davadtsat " for " dvadtsat " (twenty), and when I wondered in perplexity where to go and what to do here, and when I inevitably met Russians as disappointed as I was, I began to feel vexed and ashamed. There is a calm bay there full of steamers and boats with coloured sails. From there I could see Fiume and the distant islands covered with lilac mist, and it would have been picturesque if the view over the bay had not been hemmed in by the hotels and their *dépendances* — buildings in an absurd, trivial style of architecture, with which the whole of that green shore has been covered by greedy money grubbers, so that for the most part you see nothing in this little paradise but windows, terraces, and little squares with tables and waiters' black coats. There is a park such as you find now in every watering-place abroad. And the dark, motionless, silent foliage of the palms, and the bright yellow sand in the avenue, and the bright green seats, and the glitter of the braying military horns — all this sickened me in ten minutes! And yet one is obliged for some reason to spend ten days, ten weeks, there!

Having been dragged reluctantly from one of these watering-places to another, I have been more and more struck by the inconvenient and niggardly life led by the wealthy and well-fed, the dulness and feebleness of their imagination, the lack of boldness in their tastes and desires. And how much happier are those tourists, old and young, who, not having the money to stay in hotels, live where they can, admire the view of the sea from the tops of the mountains, lying on the green grass, walk instead of riding, see the forests and villages at close quarters, observe the customs of the country, listen to its songs, fall in love with its women. . . .

While I was sitting in the park, it began to get dark, and in the twilight my Ariadne appeared, ele-

gant and dressed like a princess; after her walked
Lubkov, wearing a new loose-fitting suit, bought
probably in Vienna.

"Why are you cross with me?" he was saying.
"What have I done to you?"

Seeing me, she uttered a cry of joy, and probably,
if we had not been in the park, would have thrown
herself on my neck. She pressed my hands warmly
and laughed; and I laughed too and almost cried
with emotion. Questions followed, of the village,
of my father, whether I had seen her brother, and
so on. She insisted on my looking her straight in
the face, and asked if I remembered the gudgeon,
our little quarrels, the picnics. . . .

"How nice it all was really!" she sighed. "But
we're not having a slow time here either. We have
a great many acquaintances, my dear, my best of
friends! To-morrow I will introduce you to a
Russian family here, but please buy yourself another
hat." She scrutinised me and frowned. "Abbazzia is not the country," she said; "here one must
be *comme il faut.*"

Then we went to the restaurant. Ariadne was
laughing and mischievous all the time; she kept calling me "dear," "good," "clever," and seemed as
though she could not believe her eyes that I was
with her. We sat on till eleven o'clock, and parted
very well satisfied both with the supper and with
each other.

Next day Ariadne presented me to the Russian

family as: " The son of a distinguished professor whose estate is next to ours."

She talked to this family about nothing but estates and crops, and kept appealing to me. She wanted to appear to be a very wealthy landowner, and did, in fact, succeed in doing so. Her manner was superb like that of a real aristocrat, which indeed she was by birth.

" But what a person my aunt is! " she said suddenly, looking at me with a smile. " We had a slight tiff, and she has bolted off to Meran. What do you say to that? "

Afterwards when we were walking in the park I asked her:

" What aunt were you talking of just now? What aunt is that? "

" That was a saving lie," laughed Ariadne. " They must not know I'm without a chaperon."

After a moment's silence she came closer to me and said:

" My dear, my dear, do be friends with Lubkov. He is so unhappy! His wife and mother are simply awful."

She used the formal mode of address in speaking to Lubkov, and when she was going up to bed she said good-night to him exactly as she did to me, and their rooms were on different floors. All this made me hope that it was all nonsense, and that there was no sort of love affair between them, and I felt at ease when I met him. And when one day he asked me for the loan of three hundred roubles, I gave it to him with the greatest pleasure.

Every day we spent in enjoying ourselves and in nothing but enjoying ourselves; we strolled in the park, we ate, we drank. Every day there were conversations with the Russian family. By degrees I got used to the fact that if I went into the park I should be sure to meet the old man with jaundice, the Catholic priest, and the Austrian General, who always carried a pack of little cards, and wherever it was possible sat down and played patience, nervously twitching his shoulders. And the band played the same thing over and over again.

At home in the country I used to feel ashamed to meet the peasants when I was fishing or on a picnic party on a working day; here too I was ashamed at the sight of the footmen, the coachmen, and the workmen who met us. It always seemed to me they were looking at me and thinking: " Why are you doing nothing? " And I was conscious of this feeling of shame every day from morning to night. It was a strange, unpleasant, monotonous time; it was only varied by Lubkov's borrowing from me now a hundred, now fifty guldens, and being suddenly revived by the money as a morphia-maniac is by morphia, beginning to laugh loudly at his wife, at himself, at his creditors.

At last it began to be rainy and cold. We went to Italy, and I telegraphed to my father begging him for mercy's sake to send me eight hundred roubles to Rome. We stayed in Venice, in Bologna, in Florence, and in every town invariably put up at an expensive hotel, where we were charged separately for lights, and for service, and for heating, and for bread at lunch, and for the right of having dinner by ourselves. We ate enormously. In the morning they gave us *café complet;* at one o'clock lunch: meat, fish, some sort of omelette, cheese, fruits, and wine. At six o'clock dinner of eight courses with long intervals, during which we drank beer and wine. At nine o'clock tea. At midnight Ariadne would declare she was hungry, and ask for ham and boiled eggs. We would eat to keep her company.

In the intervals between meals we used to rush about the museums and exhibitions in continual anxiety for fear we should be late for dinner or lunch. I was bored at the sight of the pictures; I longed to be at home to rest; I was exhausted, looked about for a chair and hypocritically repeated after other people: "How exquisite, what atmosphere!" Like overfed boa constrictors, we noticed only the most glaring objects. The shop windows hypnotised us; we went into ecstasies over imitation brooches and bought a mass of useless trumpery.

The same thing happened in Rome, where it rained and there was a cold wind. After a heavy lunch we went to look at St. Peter's, and thanks to our replete condition and perhaps the bad weather, it made no sort of impression on us, and detecting

in each other an indifference to art, we almost quar-
relled.

The money came from my father. I went to get
it, I remember, in the morning. Lubkov went with
me.

"The present cannot be full and happy when
one has a past," said he. "I have heavy burdens
left on me by the past. However, if only I get the
money, it's no great matter, but if not, I'm in a
fix. Would you believe it, I have only eight francs
left, yet I must send my wife a hundred and my
mother another. And we must live here too.
Ariadne's like a child; she won't enter into the position, and flings away money like a duchess. Why
did she buy a watch yesterday? And, tell me, what
object is there in our going on playing at being good
children? Why, our hiding our relations from the
servants and our friends costs us from ten to fifteen
francs a day, as I have to have a separate room.
What's the object of it?"

I felt as though a sharp stone had been turned
round in my chest. There was no uncertainty now;
it was all clear to me. I turned cold all over,
and at once made a resolution to give up seeing them,
to run away from them, to go home at once. . . .

"To get on terms with a woman is easy enough,"
Lubkov went on. "You have only to undress her;
but afterwards what a bore it is, what a silly business!"

When I counted over the money I received he said:

"If you don't lend me a thousand francs, I am faced with complete ruin. Your money is the only resource left to me."

I gave him the money, and he at once revived and began laughing about his uncle, a queer fish, who could never keep his address secret from his wife. When I reached the hotel I packed and paid my bill. I had still to say good-bye to Ariadne.

I knocked at the door.

"Entrez!"

In her room was the usual morning disorder: tea-things on the table, an unfinished roll, an eggshell; a strong overpowering reek of scent. The bed had not been made, and it was evident that two had slept in it.

Ariadne herself had only just got out of bed and was now with her hair down in a flannel dressing-jacket.

I said good-morning to her, and then sat in silence for a minute while she tried to put her hair tidy, and then I asked her, trembling all over:

"Why . . . why . . . did you send for me here?"

Evidently she guessed what I was thinking; she took me by the hand and said:

"I want you to be here, you are so pure."

I felt ashamed of my emotion, of my trembling.

And I was afraid I might begin sobbing, too! I went out without saying another word, and within an hour I was sitting in the train. All the journey, for some reason, I imagined Ariadne with child, and she seemed disgusting to me, and all the women I saw in the trains and at the stations looked to me, for some reason, as if they too were with child, and they too seemed disgusting and pitiable. I was in the position of a greedy, passionate miser who should suddenly discover that all his gold coins were false. The pure, gracious images which my imagination, warmed by love, had cherished for so long, my plans, my hopes, my memories, my ideas of love and of woman — all now were jeering and putting out their tongues at me. "Ariadne," I kept asking with horror, "that young, intellectual, extraordinarily beautiful girl, the daughter of a senator, carrying on an intrigue with such an ordinary, uninteresting vulgarian? But why should she not love Lubkov?" I answered myself. "In what is he inferior to me? Oh, let her love any one she likes, but why lie to me? But why is she bound to be open with me?" And so I went on over and over again till I was stupefied.

It was cold in the train; I was travelling first class, but even so there were three on a side, there were no double windows, the outer door opened straight into the compartment, and I felt as though I were in the stocks, cramped, abandoned, pitiful, and my legs were fearfully numb, and at the same time I kept recalling how fascinating she had been that morning in her dressing-jacket and with her hair down, and I was suddenly overcome by such acute jealousy that I leapt up in anguish, so that my neighbours stared at me in wonder and positive alarm.

At home I found deep snow and twenty degrees of frost. I'm fond of the winter; I'm fond of it because at that time, even in the hardest frosts, it's particularly snug at home. It's pleasant to put on one's fur jacket and felt overboots on a clear frosty day, to do something in the garden or in the yard, or to read in a well warmed room, to sit in my father's study before the open fire, to wash in my country bath-house. . . . Only if there is no mother in the house, no sister and no children, it is somehow dreary on winter evenings, and they seem extraordinarily long and quiet. And the warmer and snugger it is, the more acutely is this lack felt. In the winter when I came back from abroad, the evenings were endlessly long, I was intensely depressed, so depressed that I could not even read; in the daytime I was coming and going, clearing away the snow in the garden or feeding the chickens and the calves, but in the evening it was all up with me.

I had never cared for visitors before, but now I was glad of them, for I knew there was sure to be talk of Ariadne. Kotlovitch, the spiritualist, used often to come to talk about his sister, and sometimes he brought with him his friend Prince Maktuev, who was as much in love with Ariadne as I was. To sit in Ariadne's room, to finger the keys of her piano, to look at her music was a necessity for the prince — he could not live without it; and the spirit of his grandfather Ilarion was still predicting that sooner or later she would be his wife. The prince usually stayed a long time with us, from lunch to midnight, saying nothing all the time; in silence he would drink two or three bottles of beer, and from time to time, to show that he too was taking part in the conversation, he would laugh an abrupt, melancholy, foolish laugh. Before going home he would always take me aside and ask me in an undertone: "When did you see Ariadne Grigoryevna last? Was she quite well? I suppose she's not tired of being out there?"

Spring came on. There was the harrowing to do and then the sowing of spring corn and clover. I was sad, but there was the feeling of spring. One longed to accept the inevitable. Working in the fields and listening to the larks, I asked myself: "Couldn't I have done with this question of personal happiness once and for all? Couldn't I lay aside my fancy and marry a simple peasant girl?"

Suddenly when we were at our very busiest, I got a letter with the Italian stamp, and the clover and the beehives and the calves and the peasant girl all floated away like smoke. This time Ariadne wrote that she was profoundly, infinitely unhappy. She reproached me for not holding out a helping hand to her, for looking down upon her from the heights of my virtue and deserting her at the moment of danger. All this was written in a large, nervous handwriting with blots and smudges, and it was evident that she wrote in haste and distress. In conclusion she besought me to come and save her. Again my anchor was hauled up and I was carried away. Ariadne was in Rome. I arrived late in the evening, and when she saw me, she sobbed and threw herself on my neck. She had not changed at all that winter, and was just as young and charming. We had supper together and afterwards drove about Rome until dawn, and all the time she kept telling me about her doings. I asked where Lubkov was.

"Don't remind me of that creature!" she cried. "He is loathsome and disgusting to me!"

"But I thought you loved him," I said.

"Never," she said. "At first he struck me as original and aroused my pity, that was all. He is insolent and takes a woman by storm. And that's attractive. But we won't talk about him. That is a melancholy page in my life. He has gone to Russia to get money. Serve him right! I told him not to dare to come back."

She was living then, not at an hotel, but in a private lodging of two rooms which she had decorated in her own taste, frigidly and luxuriously. After Lubkov had gone away she had borrowed from her acquaintances about five thousand francs, and my arrival certainly was the one salvation for her. I had reckoned on taking her back to the country,

but I did not succeed in that.   She was homesick
for her native place, but her recollections of the poverty she had been through there, of privations, of
the rusty roof on her brother's house, roused a shud-
der of disgust, and when I suggested going home to
her, she squeezed my hands convulsively and said:

"No, no, I shall die of boredom there!"

Then my love entered upon its final phase.

"Be the darling that you used to be; love me a
little," said Ariadne, bending over to me.   "You're
sulky and prudent, you're afraid to yield to impulse, and keep thinking of consequences, and that's
dull.   Come, I beg you, I beseech you, be nice to
me! . . . My pure one, my holy one, my dear one,
I love you so!"

I became her lover.   For a month anyway I was
like a madman, conscious of nothing but rapture.
To hold in one's arms a young and lovely body, with
bliss to feel her warmth every time one waked up
from sleep, and to remember that she was there —
she, my Ariadne! — oh, it was not easy to get used
to that!   But yet I did get used to it, and by degrees
became capable of reflecting on. my new position.
First of all, I realised, as before, that Ariadne did
not love me.   But she wanted to be really in love,
she was afraid of solitude, and, above all, I was
healthy, young, vigorous; she was sensual, like all
cold people, as a rule — and we both made a show
of being united by a passionate, mutual love.   Afterwards I realised something else, too.

We stayed in Rome, in Naples, in Florence; we went to Paris, but there we thought it cold and went back to Italy.   We introduced ourselves everywhere as husband and wife, wealthy landowners.   People readily made our acquaintance and Ariadne had great social success everywhere.   As she took lessons in painting, she was called an artist, and only imagine, that quite suited her, though she had not the slightest trace of talent.

She would sleep every day till two or three o'clock; she had her coffee and lunch in bed.   At dinner she would eat soup, lobster, fish, meat, asparagus, game, and after she had gone to bed I used to bring up something, for instance roast beef, and she would eat it with a melancholy, careworn expression, and if she waked in the night she would eat apples and oranges.

The chief, so to say fundamental, characteristic of the woman was an amazing duplicity.   She was continually deceitful every minute, apparently apart from any necessity, as it were by instinct, by an impulse such as makes the sparrow chirrup and the cockroach waggle its antennæ.   She was deceitful with me, with the footman, with the porter, with the tradesmen in the shops, with her acquaintances; not one conversation, not one meeting, took place without affectation and pretence.   A man had only to come into our room — whoever it might be, a waiter, or a baron — for her eyes, her expression, her voice to change, even the contour of her figure

was transformed.   At the very first glance at her
then, you would have said there were no more
wealthy and fashionable people in Italy than we.
She never met an artist or a musician without telling
him all sorts of lies about his remarkable talent.

"You have such a talent!" she would say, in
honeyed cadences, "I'm really afraid of you.   I
think you must see right through people."

And all this simply in order to please, to be successful, to be fascinating!   She waked up every
morning with the one thought of "pleasing"!   It
was the aim and object of her life.   If I had told
her that in such a house, in such a street, there lived
a man who was not attracted by her, it would have
caused her real suffering.   She wanted every day
to enchant, to captivate, to drive men crazy.   The
fact that I was in her power and reduced to a complete nonentity before her charms gave her the same
sort of satisfaction that visitors used to feel in tour-
naments.   My subjection was not enough, and at
nights, stretched out like a tigress, uncovered — she
was always too hot — she would read the letters sent
her by Lubkov; he besought her to return to Russia, vowing if she did not he would rob or murder
some one to get the money to come to her.   She hated
him, but his passionate, slavish letters excited her.
She had an extraordinary opinion of her own charms;
she imagined that if somewhere, in some great assembly, men could have seen how beautifully she
was made and the colour of her skin, she would have

vanquished all Italy, the whole world. Her talk
of her figure, of her skin, offended me, and observing
this, she would, when she was angry, to vex me, say
all sorts of vulgar things, taunting me. One day
when we were at the summer villa of a lady of our
acquaintance, and she lost her temper, she even went
so far as to say: "If you don't leave off boring
me with your sermons, I'll undress this minute and
lie naked here on these flowers."

Often looking at her asleep, or eating, or trying
to assume a naïve expression, I wondered why that
extraordinary beauty, grace, and intelligence had
been given her by God. Could it simply be for
lolling in bed, eating and lying, lying endlessly?
And was she intelligent really? She was afraid of
three candles in a row, of the number thirteen, was
terrified of spells and bad dreams. She argued
about free love and freedom in general like a big-
oted old woman, declared that Boleslav Markevitch
was a better writer than Turgenev. But she was
diabolically cunning and sharp, and knew how to
seem a highly educated, advanced person in company.

Even at a good-humoured moment, she could always insult a servant or kill an insect without a pang;
she liked bull-fights, liked to read about murders,
and was angry when prisoners were acquitted.

For the life Ariadne and I were leading, we had
to have a great deal of money. My poor father
sent me his pension, all the little sums he received,

borrowed for me wherever he could, and when one day he answered me: " Non habeo," I sent him a desperate telegram in which I besought him to mortgage the estate.   A little later I begged him to get money somehow on a second mortgage.   He did this too without a murmur and sent me every farthing.   Ariadne despised the practical side of life; all this was no concern of hers, and when flinging away thousands of francs to satisfy her mad desires I groaned like an old tree, she would be singing " Addio bella Napoli " with a light heart.

Little by little I grew cold to her and began to be ashamed of our tie.   I am not fond of pregnancy and confinements, but now I sometimes dreamed of a child who would have been at least a formal justification of our life.   That I might not be completely disgusted with myself, I began reading and visiting museums and galleries, gave up drinking and took to eating very little.   If one keeps oneself well in hand from morning to night, one's heart seems lighter.   I began to bore Ariadne too.   The people with whom she won her triumphs were, by the way, all of the middling sort; as before, there were no ambassadors, there was no salon, the money did not run to it, and this mortified her and made her sob, and she announced to me at last that perhaps she would not be against our returning to Russia.

And here we are on our way.   For the last few months she has been zealously corresponding with her brother; she evidently has some secret projects,

but what they are — God knows! I am sick of trying to fathom her underhand schemes! But we're
going, not to the country, but to Yalta and afterwards to the Caucasus. She can only exist now at
watering-places, and if you knew how I hate all these
watering-places, how suffocated and ashamed I am in
them. If I could be in the country now! If I could
only be working now, earning my bread by the sweat
of my brow, atoning for my follies. I am conscious
of a superabundance of energy and I believe that if
I were to put that energy to work I could redeem
my estate in five years. But now, as you see, there
is a complication. Here we're not abroad, but in
mother Russia; we shall have to think of lawful wed-
lock. Of course, all attraction is over; there is no
trace left of my old love, but, however that may be, I
am bound in honour to marry her.

   .   .   .   .

Shamohin, excited by his story, went below with
me and we continued talking about women. It was
late. It appeared that he and I were in the same
cabin.

" So far it is only in the village that woman has
not fallen behind man," said Shamohin. " There
she thinks and feels just as man does, and struggles
with nature in the name of culture as zealously as
he. In the towns the woman of the bourgeois or intellectual class has long since fallen behind, and is
returning to her primitive condition. She is half
a human beast already, and, thanks to her, a great

deal of what had been won by human genius has been lost again; the woman gradually disappears and in her place is the primitive female. This dropping-back on the part of the educated woman is a real danger to culture; in her retrogressive movement she tries to drag man after her and prevents him from moving forward. That is incontestable."

I asked: "Why generalise? Why judge of all women from Ariadne alone? The very struggle of women for education and sexual equality, which I look upon as a struggle for justice, precludes any hypothesis of a retrograde movement."

But Shamohin scarcely listened to me and he smiled distrustfully. He was a passionate, convinced misogynist, and it was impossible to alter his convictions.

"Oh, nonsense!" he interrupted. "When once a woman sees in me, not a man, not an equal, but a male, and her one anxiety all her life is to attract me — that is, to take possession of me — how can one talk of their rights? Oh, don't you believe them; they are very, very cunning! We men make a great stir about their emancipation, but they don't care about their emancipation at all, they only pretend to care about it; they are horribly cunning things, horribly cunning!"

I began to feel sleepy and weary of discussion. I turned over with my face to the wall.

"Yes," I heard as I fell asleep —"yes, and it's our education that's at fault, sir. In our towns, the whole education and bringing up of women in its essence tends to develop her into the human beast — that is, to make her attractive to the male and able to vanquish him. Yes, indeed "— Shamohin sighed —" little girls ought to be taught and brought up with boys, so that they might be always together. A woman ought to be trained so that she may be able, like a man, to recognise when she's wrong, or she always thinks she's in the right. Instil into a little girl from her cradle that a man is not first of all a cavalier or a possible lover, but her neighbour, her equal in everything. Train her to think logically, to generalise, and do not assure her that her brain weighs less than a man's and that therefore she can be indifferent to the sciences, to the arts, to the tasks of culture in general. The apprentice to the shoemaker or the house painter has a brain of smaller size than the grown-up man too, yet he works, suffers, takes his part in the general struggle for existence. We must give up our attitude to the physiological aspect, too — to pregnancy and child-birth, seeing that in the first place women don't have babies every month; secondly, not all women have babies; and, thirdly, a normal countrywoman works in the fields up to the day of her confinement and it does her no harm. Then there ought to be ab-solute equality in everyday life. If a man gives a lady his chair or picks up the handkerchief she has dropped, let her repay him in the same way. I have no objection if a girl of good family helps me to put on my coat or hands me a glass of water ——"

I heard no more, for I fell asleep.

Next morning when we were approaching Sevastopol, it was damp, unpleasant weather; the ship
rocked. Shamohin sat on deck with me, brooding
and silent. When the bell rang for tea, men with
their coat-collars turned up and ladies with pale,
sleepy faces began going below; a young and very
beautiful lady, the one who had been so angry with
the Customs officers at Volotchisk, stopped before
Shamohin and said with the expression of a naughty,
fretful child:

" Jean, your birdie's been sea-sick."

Afterwards when I was at Yalta I saw the same
beautiful lady dashing about on horseback with a
couple of officers hardly able to keep up with her.
And one morning I saw her in an overall and a
Phrygian cap, sketching on the sea-front with a great
crowd admiring her a little way off. I too was introduced to her. She pressed my hand with great
warmth, and looking at me ecstatically, thanked me
in honeyed cadences for the pleasure I had given
her by my writings.

" Don't you believe her," Shamohin whispered to
me, " she has never read a word of them."

When I was walking on the sea-front in the early
evening Shamohin met me with his arms full of
big parcels of fruits and dainties.

" Prince Maktuev is here!" he said joyfully.
" He came yesterday with her brother, the spirit-

ualist! Now I understand what she was writing to him about! Oh, Lord!" he went on, gazing up to heaven, and pressing his parcels to his bosom. "If she hits it off with the prince, it means freedom, then I can go back to the country with my father!"

And he ran on.

"I begin to believe in spirits," he called to me, looking back. "The spirit of grandfather Ilarion seems to have prophesied the truth! Oh, if only it is so!"

The day after this meeting I left Yalta and how Shamohin's story ended I don't know.

1895

POLINKA

POLINKA

It is one o'clock in the afternoon. Shopping is at its height at the "Nouveautés de Paris," a drapery establishment in one of the Arcades. There is a monotonous hum of shopmen's voices, the hum one hears at school when the teacher sets the boys to learn something by heart. This regular sound is not interrupted by the laughter of lady customers nor the slam of the glass door, nor the scurrying of the boys.

Polinka, a thin fair little person whose mother is the head of a dressmaking establishment, is standing in the middle of the shop looking about for some one. A dark-browed boy runs up to her and asks, looking at her very gravely:

"What is your pleasure, madam?"

"Nikolay Timofeitch always takes my order," answers Polinka.

Nikolay Timofeitch, a graceful dark young man, fashionably dressed, with frizzled hair and a big pin in his cravat, has already cleared a place on the counter and is craning forward, looking at Polinka with a smile.

"Morning, Pelagea Sergeevna!" he cries in a pleasant, hearty baritone voice. "What can I do for you?"

" Good-morning! " says Polinka, going up to him.
" You see, I'm back again. . . . Show me some
gimp, please."

" Gimp — for what purpose? "

" For a bodice trimming — to trim a whole dress,
in fact."

" Certainly."

Nickolay Timofeitch lays several kinds of gimp
before Polinka; she looks at the trimmings languidly and begins bargaining over them.

" Oh, come, a rouble's not dear," says the shopman persuasively, with a condescending smile.
" It's a French trimming, pure silk. . . . We have a
commoner sort, if you like, heavier.   That's forty-
five kopecks a yard; of course, it's nothing like the
same quality."

" I want a bead corselet, too, with gimp buttons,"
says Polinka, bending over the gimp and sighing for
some reason.   " And have you any bead motifs to
match? "

" Yes."

Polinka bends still lower over the counter and
asks softly:

" And why did you leave us so early on Thursday,
Nikolay Timofeitch? "

" Hm!   It's queer you noticed it," says the shopman, with a smirk.   " You were so taken up with
that fine student that . . . it's queer you noticed
it! "

Polinka flushes crimson and remains mute.   With

a nervous quiver in his fingers the shopman closes the boxes, and for no sort of object piles them one on the top of another. A moment of silence follows.

" I want some bead lace, too," says Polinka, lifting her eyes guiltily to the shopman.

" What sort? Black or coloured? Bead lace on tulle is the most fashionable trimming."

" And how much is it? "

" The black's from eighty kopecks and the coloured from two and a half roubles. I shall never come and see you again," Nikolay Timofeitch adds in an undertone.

" Why? "

" Why? It's very simple. You must understand that yourself. Why should I distress myself? It's a queer business! Do you suppose it's a pleasure to me to see that student carrying on with you? I see it all and I understand. Even since autumn he's been hanging about you and you go for a walk with him almost every day; and when he is with you, you gaze at him as though he were an angel. You are in love with him; there's no one to beat him in your eyes. Well, all right, then, it's no good talking."

Polinka remains dumb and moves her finger on the counter in embarrassment.

" I see it all," the shopman goes on. " What inducement have I to come and see you? I've got some pride. It's not every one likes to play gooseberry. What was it you asked for? "

"Mamma told me to get a lot of things, but I've forgotten. I want some feather trimming too."

"What kind would you like?"

"The best, something fashionable."

"The most fashionable now are real bird feathers. If you want the most fashionable colour, it's heliotrope or *kanak* — that is, claret with a yellow shade in it. We have an immense choice. And what all this affair is going to lead to, I really don't understand. Here you are in love, and how is it to end?"

Patches of red come into Nikolay Timofeitch's face round his eyes. He crushes the soft feather trimming in his hand and goes on muttering:

"Do you imagine he'll marry you — is that it? You'd better drop any such fancies. Students are forbidden to marry. And do you suppose he comes to see you with honourable intentions? A likely idea! Why, these fine students don't look on us as human beings . . . they only go to see shop-keepers and dressmakers to laugh at their ignorance and to drink. They're ashamed to drink at home and in good houses, but with simple uneducated people like us they don't care what any one thinks; they'd be ready to stand on their heads. Yes! Well, which feather trimming will you take? And if he hangs about and carries on with you, we know what he is after. . . . When he's a doctor or a lawyer he'll remember you: 'Ah,' he'll say, 'I used to have a pretty fair little thing! I wonder where she is now?' Even now I bet you he boasts among his friends that he's got his eye on a little dressmaker."

Polinka sits down and gazes pensively at the pile of white boxes.

"No, I won't take the feather trimming," she sighs. "Mamma had better choose it for herself; I may get the wrong one. I want six yards of fringe for an overcoat, at forty kopecks the yard. For the same coat I want cocoa-nut buttons, perforated, so they can be sown on firmly. . . ."

Nikolay Timofeitch wraps up the fringe and the buttons. She looks at him guiltily and evidently expects him to go on talking, but he remains sullenly silent while he tidies up the feather trimming.

"I mustn't forget some buttons for a dressing-gown . . ." she says after an interval of silence, wiping her pale lips with a handkerchief.

"What kind?"

"It's for a shopkeeper's wife, so give me something rather striking."

"Yes, if it's for a shopkeeper's wife, you'd better have something bright. Here are some buttons. A combination of colours — red, blue, and the fashionable gold shade. Very glaring. The more refined prefer dull black with a bright border. But I don't understand. Can't you see for yourself? What can these . . . walks lead to?"

"I don't know," whispers Polinka, and she bends over the buttons; "I don't know myself what's come to me, Nikolay Timofeitch."

A solid shopman with whiskers forces his way

behind Nikolay Timofeitch's back, squeezing him
to the counter, and beaming with the choicest gal-
lantry, shouts:

" Be so kind, madam, as to step into this department. We have three kinds of jerseys: plain,
braided, and trimmed with beads! Which may I
have the pleasure of showing you? "

At the same time a stout lady passes by Polinka,
pronouncing in a rich, deep voice, almost a bass:

" They must be seamless, with the trade mark
stamped in them, please."

" Pretend to be looking at the things," Nikolay
Timofeitch whispers, bending down to Polinka with
a forced smile. " Dear me, you do look pale and
ill; you are quite changed. He'll throw you over,
Pelagea Sergeevna! Or if he does marry you, it
won't be for love but from hunger; he'll be tempted
by your money. He'll furnish himself a nice home
with your dowry, and then be ashamed of you.
He'll keep you out of sight of his friends and visitors, because you're uneducated. He'll call you ' my
dummy of a wife.' You wouldn't know how to behave in a doctor's or lawyer's circle. To them you're
a dressmaker, an ignorant creature."

" Nikolay Timofeitch! " somebody shouts from
the other end of the shop. " The young lady here
wants three yards of ribbon with a metal stripe.
Have we any? "

Nikolay Timofeitch turns in that direction, smirks
and shouts:

"Yes, we have! Ribbon with a metal stripe, ottoman with a satin stripe, and satin with a moiré stripe!"

"Oh, by the way, I mustn't forget, Olga asked me to get her a pair of stays!" says Polinka.

"There are tears in your eyes," says Nikolay Timofeitch in dismay. "What's that for? Come to the corset department, I'll screen you — it looks awkward."

With a forced smile and exaggeratedly free and easy manner, the shopman rapidly conducts Polinka to the corset department and conceals her from the public eye behind a high pyramid of boxes.

"What sort of corset may I show you?" he asks aloud, whispering immediately: "Wipe your eyes!"

"I want . . . I want . . . size forty-eight centimetres. Only she wanted one, lined . . . with real whalebone . . . I must talk to you, Nikolay Timofeitch. Come to-day!"

"Talk? What about? There's nothing to talk about."

"You are the only person who . . . cares about me, and I've no one to talk to but you."

"These are not reed or steel, but real whalebone. . . . What is there for us to talk about? It's no use talking. . . . You are going for a walk with him to-day, I suppose?"

"Yes; I . . . I am."

"Then what's the use of talking? Talk won't help. . . . You are in love, aren't you?"

"Yes . . ." Polinka whispers hesitatingly, and big tears gush from her eyes.

"What is there to say?" mutters Nikolay Timofeitch, shrugging his shoulders nervously and turning pale. "There's no need of talk. . . . Wipe your eyes, that's all. I . . . I ask for nothing."

At that moment a tall, lanky shopman comes up to the pyramid of boxes, and says to his customer:

"Let me show you some good elastic garters that do not impede the circulation, certified by medical authority . . ."

Nikolay Timofeitch screens Polinka, and, trying to conceal her emotion and his own, wrinkles his face into a smile and says aloud:

"There are two kinds of lace, madam: cotton and silk! Oriental, English, Valenciennes, crochet, torchon, are cotton. And rococo, soutache, Cambray, are silk. . . . For God's sake, wipe your eyes! They're coming this way!"

And seeing that her tears are still gushing he goes on louder than ever:

"Spanish, Rococo, soutache, Cambray . . . stockings, thread, cotton, silk . . ."

1887

ANYUTA

ANYUTA

In the cheapest room of a big block of furnished apartments Stepan Klotchkov, a medical student in his third year, was walking to and fro, zealously conning his anatomy. His mouth was dry and his forehead perspiring from the unceasing effort to learn it by heart.

In the window, covered by patterns of frost, sat on a stool the girl who shared his room — Anyuta, a thin little brunette of five-and-twenty, very pale with mild grey eyes. Sitting with bent back she was busy embroidering with red thread the collar of a man's shirt. She was working against time. . . . The clock in the passage struck two drowsily, yet the little room had not been put to rights for the morning. Crumpled bed-clothes, pillows thrown about, books, clothes, a big filthy slop-pail filled with soap-suds in which cigarette ends were swimming, and the litter on the floor — all seemed as though purposely jumbled together in one confusion. . . .

"The right lung consists of three parts . . ." Klotchkov repeated. "Boundaries! Upper part on anterior wall of thorax reaches the fourth or fifth rib, on the lateral surface, the fourth rib . . . behind to the *spina scapulæ* . . ."

Klotchkov raised his eyes to the ceiling, striving

to visualise what he had just read.   Unable to form
a clear picture of it, he began feeling his upper ribs
through his waistcoat.

" These ribs are like the keys of a piano," he
said.   " One must familiarise oneself with them
somehow, if one is not to get muddled over them.
One must study them in the skeleton and the living
body. . . . I say, Anyuta, let me pick them out."

Anyuta put down her sewing, took off her blouse,
and straightened herself up.   Klotchkov sat down
facing her, frowned, and began counting her ribs.

" H'm! . . . One can't feel the first rib; it's
behind the shoulder-blade. . . . This must be the
second rib. . . . Yes . . . this is the third . . .
this is the fourth. . . . H'm! . . . yes. . . . Why
are you wriggling? "

" Your fingers are cold! "

" Come, come . . . it won't kill you.   Don't
twist about.   That must be the third rib, then . . .
this is the fourth. . . . You look such a skinny
thing, and yet one can hardly feel your ribs.   That's
the second . . . that's the third. . . . Oh, this
is muddling, and one can't see it clearly. . . . I must
draw it. . . . Where's my crayon? "

Klotchkov took his crayon and drew on Anyuta's
chest several parallel lines corresponding with the
ribs.

" First-rate.   That's all straightforward. . . .
Well, now I can sound you.   Stand up! "

Anyuta stood up and raised her chin.   Klotchkov

began sounding her, and was so absorbed in this occupation that he did not notice how Anyuta's lips, nose, and fingers turned blue with cold. Anyuta shivered, and was afraid the student, noticing it, would leave off drawing and sounding her, and then, perhaps, might fail in his exam.

" Now it's all clear," said Klotchkov when he had finished. " You sit like that and don't rub off the crayon, and meanwhile I'll learn up a little more."

And the student again began walking to and fro, repeating to himself. Anyuta, with black stripes across her chest, looking as though she had been tattooed, sat thinking, huddled up and shivering with cold. She said very little as a rule; she was always silent, thinking and thinking. . . .

In the six or seven years of her wanderings from one furnished room to another, she had known five students like Klotchkov. Now they had all finished their studies, had gone out into the world, and, of course, like respectable people, had long ago forgotten her. One of them was living in Paris, two were doctors, the fourth was an artist, and the fifth was said to be already a professor. Klotchkov was the sixth. . . . Soon he, too, would finish his studies and go out into the world. There was a fine future before him, no doubt, and Klotchkov probably would become a great man, but the present was anything but bright; Klotchkov had no tobacco and no tea, and there were only four lumps of sugar left. She must make haste and finish her embroidery, take it to the woman who had ordered it, and with the quarter rouble she would get for it, buy tea and tobacco.

"Can I come in?" asked a voice at the door.

Anyuta quickly threw a woollen shawl over her shoulders.   Fetisov, the artist, walked in.

"I have come to ask you a favour," he began, addressing Klotchkov, and glaring like a wild beast from under the long locks that hung over his brow. "Do me a favour; lend me your young lady just for a couple of hours!   I'm painting a picture, you see, and I can't get on without a model."

"Oh, with pleasure," Klotchkov agreed.   "Go along, Anyuta."

"The things I've had to put up with there," Anyuta murmured softly.

"Rubbish!   The man's asking you for the sake of art, and not for any sort of nonsense.   Why not help him if you can?"

Anyuta began dressing.

"And what are you painting?" asked Klotchkov.

"Psyche; it's a fine subject.   But it won't go, somehow.   I have to keep painting from different models.   Yesterday I was painting one with blue legs.   'Why are your legs blue?' I asked her. 'It's my stockings stain them,' she said.   And you're still grinding!   Lucky fellow!   You have patience."

"Medicine's a job one can't get on with without grinding."

"H'm! . . . Excuse me, Klotchkov, but you

do live like a pig! It's awful the way you live!"

"How do you mean? I can't help it. . . . I only get twelve roubles a month from my father, and it's hard to live decently on that."

"Yes . . . yes . . ." said the artist, frowning with an air of disgust; " but, still, you might live better. . . . An educated man is in duty bound to have taste, isn't he? And goodness knows what it's like here! The bed not made, the slops, the dirt . . . yesterday's porridge in the plates. . . . Tfoo!"

"That's true," said the student in confusion; "but Anyuta has had no time to-day to tidy up; she's been busy all the while."

When Anyuta and the artist had gone out Klotchkov lay down on the sofa and began learning, lying down; then he accidentally dropped asleep, and waking up an hour later, propped his head on his fists and sank into gloomy reflection. He recalled the artist's words that an educated man was in duty bound to have taste, and his surroundings actually struck him now as loathsome and revolting. He saw, as it were in his mind's eye, his own future, when he would see his patients in his consulting-room, drink tea in a large dining-room in the company of his wife, a real lady. And now that slop-pail in which the cigarette ends were swimming looked incredibly disgusting. Anyuta, too, rose before his imagination —a plain, slovenly, pitiful figure . . . and he made up his mind to part with her at once, at all costs.

When, on coming back from the artist's, she took off her coat, he got up and said to her seriously:

"Look here, my good girl . . . sit down and listen. We must part! The fact is, I don't want to live with you any longer."

Anyuta had come back from the artist's worn out and exhausted. Standing so long as a model had made her face look thin and sunken, and her chin sharper than ever. She said nothing in answer to the student's words, only her lips began to tremble.

"You know we should have to part sooner or later, anyway," said the student. "You're a nice, good girl, and not a fool; you'll understand. . . ."

Anyuta put on her coat again, in silence wrapped up her embroidery in paper, gathered together her needles and thread: she found the screw of paper with the four lumps of sugar in the window, and laid it on the table by the books.

"That's . . . your sugar . . ." she said softly, and turned away to conceal her tears.

"Why are you crying?" asked Klotchkov.

He walked about the room in confusion, and said:

"You are a strange girl, really. . . . Why, you know we shall have to part. We can't stay together for ever."

She had gathered together all her belongings, and turned to say good-bye to him, and he felt sorry for her.

"Shall I let her stay on here another week?" he thought. "She really may as well stay, and I'll tell her to go in a week;" and vexed at his own weakness, he shouted to her roughly:

"Come, why are you standing there? If you are going, go; and if you don't want to, take off your coat and stay! You can stay!"

Anyuta took off her coat, silently, stealthily, then blew her nose also stealthily, sighed, and noiselessly returned to her invariable position on her stool by the window.

The student drew his textbook to him and began again pacing from corner to corner. "The right lung consists of three parts," he repeated; "the upper part, on anterior wall of thorax, reaches the fourth or fifth rib . . ."

In the passage some one shouted at the top of his voice: "Grigory! The samovar!"

1886

THE TWO VOLODYAS

THE TWO VOLODYAS

"LET me; I want to drive myself! I'll sit by the driver!" Sofya Lvovna said in a loud voice. "Wait a minute, driver; I'll get up on the box beside you."

She stood up in the sledge, and her husband, Vladimir Nikititch, and the friend of her childhood, Vladimir Mihalovitch, held her arms to prevent her falling. The three horses were galloping fast.

"I said you ought not to have given her brandy," Vladimir Nikititch whispered to his companion with vexation. "What a fellow you are, really!"

The Colonel knew by experience that in women like his wife, Sofya Lvovna, after a little too much wine, turbulent gaiety was followed by hysterical laughter and then tears. He was afraid that when they got home, instead of being able to sleep, he would have to be administering compresses and drops.

"Wo!" cried Sofya Lvovna. "I want to drive myself!"

She felt genuinely gay and triumphant. For the last two months, ever since her wedding, she had been tortured by the thought that she had married Colonel Yagitch from worldly motives and, as it is said, *par dépit;* but that evening, at the restaurant, she had suddenly become convinced that she loved him passionately.   In spite of his fifty-four years, he was so slim, agile, supple, he made puns and hummed to the gipsies' tunes so charmingly. Really, the older men were nowadays a thousand times more interesting than the young.   It seemed as though age and youth had changed parts.   The Colonel was two years older than her father, but could there be any importance in that if, honestly speaking, there were infinitely more vitality, go, and freshness in him than in herself, though she was only twenty-three?

"Oh, my darling!" she thought.   "You are wonderful!"

She had become convinced in the restaurant, too, that not a spark of her old feeling remained.   For the friend of her childhood, Vladimir Mihalovitch, or simply Volodya, with whom only the day before she had been madly, miserably in love, she now felt nothing but complete indifference.   All that evening he had seemed to her spiritless, torpid, uninteresting, and insignificant, and the *sangfroid* with which he habitually avoided paying at restaurants on this occasion revolted her, and she had hardly been able to resist saying, "If you are poor, you should stay at home."   The Colonel paid for all.

Perhaps because trees, telegraph posts, and drifts of snow kept flitting past her eyes, all sorts of disconnected ideas came rushing into her mind.   She reflected: the bill at the restaurant had been a hundred and twenty roubles, and a hundred had gone

to the gipsies, and to-morrow she could fling away
a thousand roubles if she liked; and only two months
ago, before her wedding, she had not had three roubles of her own, and had to ask her father for every
trifle. What a change in her life!

Her thoughts were in a tangle. She recalled, how,
when she was a child of ten, Colonel Yagitch, now
her husband, used to make love to her aunt, and
every one in the house said that he had ruined her.
And her aunt had, in fact, often come down to dinner with her eyes red from crying, and was always
going off somewhere; and people used to say of her
that the poor thing could find no peace anywhere.
He had been very handsome in those days, and had
an extraordinary reputation as a lady-killer. So
much so that he was known all over the town, and
it was said of him that he paid a round of visits to
his adorers every day like a doctor visiting his patients. And even now, in spite of his grey hair, his
wrinkles, and his spectacles, his thin face looked
handsome, especially in profile.

Sofya Lvovna's father was an army doctor, and
had at one time served in the same regiment with
Colonel Yagitch. Volodya's father was an army
doctor too, and he, too, had once been in the same
regiment as her father and Colonel Yagitch. In
spite of many amatory adventures, often very com-
plicated and disturbing, Volodya had done splendidly
at the university, and had taken a very good degree.
Now he was specialising in foreign literature, and

was said to be writing a thesis. He lived with his
father, the army doctor, in the barracks, and had
no means of his own, though he was thirty. As
children Sofya and he had lived under the same roof,
though in different flats. He often came to play
with her, and they had dancing and French lessons together. But when he grew up into a graceful, remarkably handsome young man, she began to
feel shy of him, and then fell madly in love with him,
and had loved him right up to the time when she
was married to Yagitch. He, too, had been re-
nowned for his success with women almost from the
age of fourteen, and the ladies who deceived their
husbands on his account excused themselves by saying that he was only a boy. Some one had told a
story of him lately that when he was a student living in lodgings so as to be near the university, it
always happened if one knocked at his door, that
one heard his footstep, and then a whispered apol-
ogy: " *Pardon, je ne suis pas seul.*" Yagitch was
delighted with him, and blessed him as a worthy suc-
cessor, as Derchavin blessed Pushkin; he appeared
to be fond of him. They would play billiards or
picquet by the hour together without uttering a word,
if Yagitch drove out on any expedition he always
took Volodya with him, and Yagitch was the only
person Volodya initiated into the mysteries of his
thesis. In earlier days, when Yagitch was rather
younger, they had often been in the position of rivals,
but they had never been jealous of one another. In

the circle in which they moved Yagitch was nicknamed Big Volodya, and his friend Little Volodya.

Besides Big Volodya, Little Volodya, and Sofya
Lvovna, there was a fourth person in the sledge —
Margarita Alexandrovna, or, as every one called her,
Rita, a cousin of Madame Yagitch — a very pale
girl over thirty, with black eyebrows and a pince-
nez, who was for ever smoking cigarettes, even in
the bitterest frost, and who always had her knees
and the front of her blouse covered with cigarette
ash. She spoke through her nose, drawling every
word, was of a cold temperament, could drink any
amount of wine and liquor without being drunk, and
used to tell scandalous anecdotes in a languid and
tasteless way. At home she spent her days reading
thick magazines, covering them with cigarette ash,
or eating frozen apples.

" Sonia, give over fooling," she said, drawling.
" It's really silly."

As they drew near the city gates they went more
slowly, and began to pass people and houses. Sofya
Lvovna subsided, nestled up to her husband, and
gave herself up to her thoughts. Litle Volodya sat
opposite. By now her light-hearted and cheerful
thoughts were mingled with gloomy ones. She
thought that the man sitting opposite knew that she
loved him, and no doubt he believed the gossip that
she married the Colonel *par dépit*. She had never
told him of her love; she had not wanted him to
know, and had done her best to hide her feeling, but

from her face she knew that he understood her perfectly — and her pride suffered.   But what was most humiliating in her position was that, since her wedding, Volodya had suddenly begun to pay her attention, which he had never done before, spending hours with her, sitting silent or chattering about trifles; and even now in the sledge, though he did not talk to her, he touched her foot with his and pressed her hand a little.   Evidently that was all he wanted, that she should be married; and it was evident that he despised her and that she only excited in him an interest of a special kind as though she were an immoral and disreputable woman.   And when the feeling of triumph and love for her husband were mingled in her soul with humiliation and wounded pride, she was overcome by a spirit of defiance, and longed to sit on the box, to shout and whistle to the horses.

Just as they passed the nunnery the huge hundred-ton bell rang out.   Rita crossed herself.

"Our Olga is in that nunnery," said Sofya Lvovna, and she, too, crossed herself and shuddered.

"Why did she go into the nunnery?" said the Colonel.

"*Par dépit,*" Rita answered crossly, with obvious allusion to Sofya's marrying Yagitch.   "*Par dépit* is all the fashion nowadays.   Defiance of all the world.   She was always laughing, a desperate flirt, fond of nothing but balls and young men, and all of a sudden off she went — to surprise every one!"

"That's not true," said Volodya, turning down the collar of his fur coat and showing his handsome face. "It wasn't a case of *par dépit;* it was simply horrible, if you like. Her brother Dmitri was sent to penal servitude, and they don't know where he is now. And her mother died of grief."

He turned up his collar again.

"Olga did well," he added in a muffled voice. "Living as an adopted child, and with such a paragon as Sofya Lvovna,— one must take that into consideration too!"

Sofya Lvovna heard a tone of contempt in his voice, and longed to say something rude to him, but she said nothing. The spirit of defiance came over her again; she stood up again and shouted in a tearful voice:

"I want to go to the early service! Driver, back! I want to see Olga."

They turned back. The nunnery bell had a deep note, and Sofya Lvovna fancied there was something in it that reminded her of Olga and her life. The other church bells began ringing too. When the driver stopped the horses, Sofya Lvovna jumped out of the sledge and, unescorted and alone, went quickly up to the gate.

"Make haste, please!" her husband called to her. "It's late already."

She went in at the dark gateway, then by the avenue that led from the gate to the chief church.

The snow crunched under her feet, and the ringing was just above her head, and seemed to vibrate through her whole being.   Here was the church door, then three steps down, and an ante-room with ikons of the saints on both sides, a fragrance of juniper and incense, another door, and a dark figure opening it and bowing very low.   The service had not yet begun.   One nun was walking by the ikon-screen and lighting the candles on the tall standard candlesticks, another was lighting the chandelier. Here and there, by the columns and the side chapels, there stood black, motionless figures.   " I suppose they must remain standing as they are now till the morning," thought Sofya Lvovna, and it seemed to her dark, cold, and dreary — drearier than a grave-yard.   She looked with a feeling of dreariness at the still, motionless figures and suddenly felt a pang at her heart.   For some reason, in one short nun, with thin shoulders and a black kerchief on her head, she recognised Olga, though when Olga went into the nunnery she had been plump and had looked taller.   Hesitating and extremely agitated, Sofya Lvovna went up to the nun, and looking over her shoulder into her face, recognised her as Olga.

" Olga ! " she cried, throwing up her hands, and could not speak from emotion.   " Olga ! "

The nun knew her at once; she raised her eye-brows in surprise, and her pale, freshly washed face, and even, it seemed, the white headcloth that she wore under her wimple, beamed with pleasure.

"What a miracle from God!" she said, and she, too, threw up her thin, pale little hands.

Sofya Lvovna hugged her and kissed her warmly, and was afraid as she did so that she might smell of spirits.

"We were just driving past, and we thought of you," she said, breathing hard, as though she had been running. "Dear me! How pale you are! I . . . I'm very glad to see you. Well, tell me how are you? Are you dull?"

Sofya Lvovna looked round at the other nuns, and went on in a subdued voice:

"There've been so many changes at home . . . you know, I'm married to Colonel Yagitch. You remember him, no doubt. . . . I am very happy with him."

"Well, thank God for that. And is your father quite well?"

"Yes, he is quite well. He often speaks of you. You must come and see us during the holidays, Olga, won't you?"

"I will come," said Olga, and she smiled. "I'll come on the second day."

Sofya Lvovna began crying, she did not know why, and for a minute she shed tears in silence, then she wiped her eyes and said:

"Rita will be very sorry not to have seen you. She is with us too. And Volodya's here. They

are close to the gate.   How pleased they'd be if
you'd come out and see them.   Let's go out to
them; the service hasn't begun yet."

"Let us," Olga agreed.   She crossed herself
three times and went out with Sofya Lvovna to the
entrance.

"So you say you're happy, Sonitchka?" she asked
when they came out at the gate.

"Very."

"Well, thank God for that."

The two Volodyas, seeing the nun, got out of the
sledge and greeted her respectfully.   Both were vis-
ibly touched by her pale face and her black monastic
dress, and both were pleased that she had remembered them and come to greet them.   That she
might not be cold, Sofya Lvovna wrapped her up
in a rug and put one half of her fur coat round her.
Her tears had relieved and purified her heart, and
she was glad that this noisy, restless, and, in reality,
impure night should unexpectedly end so purely and
serenely.   And to keep Olga by her a little longer
she suggested:

"Let us take her for a drive!   Get in, Olga;
we'll go a little way."

The men expected the nun to refuse — saints don't
dash about in three-horse sledges; but to their surprise, she consented and got into the sledge.   And
while the horses were galloping to the city gate all
were silent, and only tried to make her warm and
comfortable, and each of them was thinking of what

she had been in the past and what she was now.
Her face was now passionless, inexpressive, cold,
pale, and transparent, as though there were water,
not blood, in her veins.   And two or three years ago
she had been plump and rosy, talking about her
suitors and laughing at every trifle.

Near the city gate the sledge turned back; when
it stopped ten minutes later near the nunnery, Olga
got out of the sledge.   The bell had begun to ring
more rapidly.

" The Lord save you," said Olga, and she bowed
low as nuns do.

" Mind you come, Olga."

" I will, I will."

She went and quickly disappeared through the
gateway.   And when after that they drove on again,
Sofya Lvovna felt very sad.   Every one was silent.
She felt dispirited and weak all over.   That she
should have made a nun get into a sledge and drive
in a company hardly sober seemed to her now stupid,
tactless, and almost sacrilegious.   As the intoxication passed off, the desire to deceive herself passed
away also.   It was clear to her now that she did
not love her husband, and never could love him,
and that it all had been foolishness and nonsense.
She had married him from interested motives, because, in the words of her school friends, he was
madly rich, and because she was afraid of becoming
an old maid like Rita, and because she was sick of
her father, the doctor, and wanted to annoy Volodya.

If she could have imagined when she got married,
that it would be so oppressive, so dreadful, and so
hideous, she would not have consented to the marriage for all the wealth in the world.   But now there
was no setting it right.   She must make up her mind
to it.

They reached home.   Getting into her warm,
soft bed, and pulling the bed-clothes over her, Sofya
Lvovna recalled the dark church, the smell of incense, and the figures by the columns, and she felt
frightened at the thought that these figures would
be standing there all the while she was asleep.   The
early service would be very, very long; then there
would be " the hours," then the mass, then the service of the day. . . .

" But of course there is a God — there certainly
is a God; and I shall have to die, so that sooner or
later one must think of one's soul, of eternal life,
like Olga.   Olga is saved now; she has settled all
questions for herself. . . . But if there is no God?
Then her life is wasted.   But how is it wasted?
Why is it wasted? "

And a minute later the thought came into her
mind again:

" There is a God; death must come; one must
think of one's soul.   If Olga were to see death
before her this minute she would not be afraid.
She is prepared.   And the great thing is that she
has already solved the problem of life for herself.
There is a God . . . yes. . . . But is there no

other solution except going into a monastery? To go into the monastery means to renounce life, to spoil it . . ."

Sofya Lvovna began to feel rather frightened; she hid her head under her pillow.

" I mustn't think about it," she whispered. " I mustn't . . ."

Yagitch was walking about on the carpet in the next room with a soft jingle of spurs, thinking about something. The thought occurred to Sofya Lvovna that this man was near and dear to her only for one reason — that his name, too, was Vladimir. She sat up in bed and called tenderly:

" Volodya ! "

" What is it? " her husband responded.

" Nothing."

She lay down again. She heard a bell, perhaps the same nunnery bell. Again she thought of the vestibule and the dark figures, and thoughts of God and of inevitable death strayed through her mind, and she covered her ears that she might not hear the bell. She thought that before old age and death there would be a long, long life before her, and that day by day she would have to put up with being close to a man she did not love, who had just now come into the bedroom and was getting into bed, and would have to stifle in her heart her hopeless love for the other young, fascinating, and, as she thought, exceptional man. She looked at her husband and tried to say good-night to him, but suddenly burst out crying instead. She was vexed with herself.

"Well, now then for the music!" said Yagitch.

She was not pacified till ten o'clock in the morning. She left off crying and trembling all over, but she began to have a splitting headache. Yagitch was in haste to go to the late mass, and in the next room was grumbling at his orderly, who was helping him to dress. He came into the bedroom once with the soft jingle of his spurs to fetch something, and then a second time wearing his epaulettes, and his orders on his breast, limping slightly from rheumatism; and it struck Sofya Lvovna that he looked and walked like a bird of prey.

She heard Yagitch ring the telephone bell.

"Be so good as to put me on to the Vassilevsky barracks," he said; and a minute later: "Vassilevsky barracks? Please ask Doctor Salimovitch to come to the telephone . . ." And a minute later: "With whom am I speaking? Is it you, Volodya? Delighted. Ask your father to come to us at once, dear boy; my wife is rather shattered after yesterday. Not at home, you say? H'm! . . . Thank you. Very good. I shall be much obliged. . . . *Merci.*"

Yagitch came into the bedroom for the third time, bent down to his wife, made the sign of the cross over her, gave her his hand to kiss (the women who had been in love with him used to kiss his hand and he had got into the habit of it), and saying that he should be back to dinner, went out.

At twelve o'clock the maid came in to announce that Vladimir Mihalovitch had arrived. Sofya Lvovna, staggering with fatigue and headache, hurriedly put on her marvellous new lilac dressing-gown trimmed with fur, and hastily did up her hair after a fashion. She was conscious of an inexpressible tenderness in her heart, and was trembling with joy and with fear that he might go away. She wanted nothing but to look at him.

Volodya came dressed correctly for calling, in a swallow-tail coat and white tie. When Sofya Lvovna came in he kissed her hand and expressed his genuine regret that she was ill. Then when they had sat down, he admired her dressing-gown.

"I was upset by seeing Olga yesterday," she said. "At first I felt it dreadful, but now I envy her. She is like a rock that cannot be shattered; there is no moving her. But was there no other solution for her, Volodya? Is burying oneself alive the only solution of the problem of life? Why, it's death, not life!"

At the thought of Olga, Volodya's face softened.

"Here, you are a clever man, Volodya," said Sofya Lvovna. "Show me how to do what Olga has done. Of course, I am not a believer and should not go into a nunnery, but one can do something equivalent. Life isn't easy for me," she added after a brief pause. "Tell me what to do. . . . Tell me something I can believe in. Tell me something, if it's only one word."

"One word?   By all means: tararaboomdeeay."

"Volodya, why do you despise me?" she asked hotly.   "You talk to me in a special, fatuous way, if you'll excuse me, not as one talks to one's friends and women one respects.   You are so good at your work, you are fond of science; why do you never talk of it to me?   Why is it?   Am I not good enough?"

Volodya frowned with annoyance and said:

"Why do you want science all of a sudden? Don't you perhaps want constitutional government? Or sturgeon and horse-radish?"

"Very well, I am a worthless, trivial, silly woman with no convictions.   I have a mass, a mass of defects.   I am neurotic, corrupt, and I ought to be despised for it.   But you, Volodya, are ten years older than I am, and my husband is thirty years older.   I've grown up before your eyes, and if you would, you could have made anything you liked of me — an angel.   But you "— her voice quivered — "treat me horribly.   Yagitch has married me in his old age, and you . . ."

"Come, come," said Volodya, sitting nearer her and kissing both her hands.   "Let the Schopenhauers philosophise and prove whatever they like, while we'll kiss these little hands."

"You despise me, and if only you knew how miserable it makes me," she said uncertainly, knowing beforehand that he would not believe her.   "And if you only knew how I want to change, to begin another life! I think of it with enthusiasm!" and tears of enthusiasm actually came into her eyes. "To be good, honest, pure, not to be lying; to have an object in life."

"Come, come, come, please don't be affected! I don't like it!" said Volodya, and an ill-humoured expression came into his face. "Upon my word, you might be on the stage. Let us behave like simple people."

To prevent him from getting cross and going away, she began defending herself, and forced herself to smile to please him; and again she began talking of Olga, and of how she longed to solve the problem of her life and to become something real.

"Ta-ra-ra-boomdee-ay," he hummed. "Tara-ra-boom-dee-ay!"

And all at once he put his arm round her waist, while she, without knowing what she was doing, laid her hands on his shoulders and for a minute gazed with ecstasy, almost intoxication, at his clever, ironical face, his brow, his eyes, his handsome beard.

"You have known that I love you for ever so long," she confessed to him, and she blushed painfully, and felt that her lips were twitching with shame. "I love you. Why do you torture me?"

She shut her eyes and kissed him passionately on the lips, and for a long while, a full minute, could not take her lips away, though she knew it was unseemly, that he might be thinking the worse of her, that a servant might come in.

"Oh, how you torture me!" she repeated.

When half an hour later, having got all that he wanted, he was sitting at lunch in the dining-room, she was kneeling before him, gazing greedily into his face, and he told her that she was like a little dog waiting for a bit of ham to be thrown to it. Then he sat her on his knee, and dancing her up and down like a child, hummed:

"Tara-raboom-dee-ay. . . . Tara-raboomdee-ay."

And when he was getting ready to go she asked him in a passionate whisper:

"When? To-day? Where?" And held out both hands to his mouth as though she wanted to seize his answer in them.

"To-day it will hardly be convenient," he said after a minute's thought. "To-morrow, perhaps."

And they parted. Before dinner Sofya Lvovna went to the nunnery to see Olga, but there she was told that Olga was reading the psalter somewhere over the dead. From the nunnery she went to her father's and found that he, too, was out. Then she took another sledge and drove aimlessly about the streets till evening. And for some reason she kept thinking of the aunt whose eyes were red with crying, and who could find no peace anywhere.

And at night they drove out again with three horses to a restaurant out of town and listened to the gipsies. And driving back past the nunnery again, Sofya Lvovna thought of Olga, and she felt aghast at the thought that for the girls and women of her class there was no solution but to go on driving about and telling lies, or going into a nunnery to mortify the flesh. . . . And next day she met her lover, and again Sofya Lvovna drove about the town alone in a hired sledge thinking about her aunt.

A week later Volodya threw her over.   And after that life went on as before, uninteresting, miserable, and sometimes even agonising.   The Colonel and Volodya spent hours playing billiards and picquet, Rita told anecdotes in the same languid, tasteless way, and Sofya Lvovna went about alone in hired sledges and kept begging her husband to take her for a good drive with three horses.

Going almost every day to the nunnery, she wearied Olga, complaining of her unbearable misery, weeping, and feeling as she did so that she brought with her into the cell something impure, pitiful, shabby.   And Olga repeated to her mechanically as though a lesson learnt by rote, that all this was of no consequence, that it would all pass and God would forgive her.

1893

THE TROUSSEAU

THE TROUSSEAU

I HAVE seen a great many houses in my time, little
and big, new and old, built of stone and of wood,
but of one house I have kept a very vivid memory.
It was, properly speaking, rather a cottage than a
house — a tiny cottage of one story, with three windows, looking extraordinarily like a little old hunch-
back woman with a cap on.   Its white stucco walls,
its tiled roof, and dilapidated chimney, were all
drowned in a perfect sea of green.   The cottage
was lost to sight among the mulberry-trees, acacias,
and poplars planted by the grandfathers and great-
grandfathers of its present occupants.   And yet it
is a town house.   Its wide courtyard stands in a row
with other similar green courtyards, and forms part
of a street.   Nothing ever drives down that street,
and very few persons are ever seen walking through
it.

The shutters of the little house are always closed;
its occupants do not care for sunlight — the light
is no use to them.   The windows are never opened,
for they are not fond of fresh air.   People who
spend their lives in the midst of acacias, mulberries,
and nettles have no passion for nature.   It is only
to the summer visitor that God has vouchsafed an
eye for the beauties of nature.   The rest of man-

kind remain steeped in profound ignorance of the existence of such beauties.   People never prize what they have always had in abundance.   "What we have, we do not treasure," and what's more we do not even love it.

The little house stands in an earthly paradise of green trees with happy birds nesting in them. But inside . . . alas . . . !   In summer, it is close and stifling within; in winter, hot as a Turkish bath, not one breath of air, and the dreariness! . . .

The first time I visited the little house was many years ago on business.   I brought a message from the Colonel who was the owner of the house to his wife and daughter.   That first visit I remember very distinctly.   It would be impossible, indeed, to forget it.

Imagine a limp little woman of forty, gazing at you with alarm and astonishment while you walk from the passage into the parlour.   You are a stranger, a visitor, "a young man"; that's enough to reduce her to a state of terror and bewilderment. Though you have no dagger, axe, or revolver in your hand, and though you smile affably, you are met with alarm.

"Whom have I the honour and pleasure of addressing?" the little lady asks in a trembling voice.

I introduced myself and explained why I had come.

The alarm and amazement were at once succeeded by a shrill, joyful "Ach!" and she turned her eyes upwards to the ceiling.   This "Ach!" was

caught up like an echo and repeated from the hall
to the parlour, from the parlour to the kitchen, and
so on down to the cellar. Soon the whole house was
resounding with " Ach! " in various voices.

Five minutes later I was sitting on a big, soft,
warm lounge in the drawing-room listening to the
" Ach! " echoing all down the street. There was
a smell of moth powder, and of goatskin shoes, a
pair of which lay on a chair beside me wrapped in
a handkerchief. In the windows were geraniums,
and muslin curtains, and on the curtains were torpid
flies. On the wall hung the portrait of some bishop,
painted in oils, with the glass broken at one corner,
and next to the bishop a row of ancestors with lemon-
coloured faces of a gipsy type. On the table lay
a thimble, a reel of cotton, and a half-knitted stock-
ing, and paper patterns and a black blouse, tacked
together, were lying on the floor. In the next room
two alarmed and fluttered old women were hurriedly
picking up similar patterns and pieces of tailor's
chalk from the floor.

" You must, please, excuse us; we are dreadfully
untidy," said the little lady.

While she talked to me, she stole embarrassed
glances towards the other room where the patterns
were still being picked up. The door, too, seemed
embarrassed, opening an inch or two and then shut-
ting again.

" What's the matter? " said the little lady, addressing the door.

"*Où est mon cravatte lequel mon père m'avait envoyé de Koursk?*" asked a female voice at the door.

"*Ah, est-ce que, Marie . . . que.* . . . Really, it's impossible. . . . *Nous avons donc chez nous un homme peu connu de nous.* Ask Lukerya."

"How well we speak French, though!" I read in the eyes of the little lady, who was flushing with pleasure.

Soon afterwards the door opened and I saw a tall, thin girl of nineteen, in a long muslin dress with a gilt belt from which, I remember, hung a mother-of-pearl fan. She came in, dropped a curtsy, and flushed crimson. Her long nose, which was slightly pitted with smallpox, turned red first, and then the flush passed up to her eyes and her forehead.

"My daughter," chanted the little lady, "and, Manetchka, this is a young gentleman who has come," etc.

I was introduced, and expressed my surprise at the number of paper patterns. Mother and daughter dropped their eyes.

"We had a fair here at Ascension," said the mother; "we always buy materials at the fair, and then it keeps us busy with sewing till the next year's fair comes around again. We never put things out to be made. My husband's pay is not very ample, and we are not able to permit ourselves luxuries. So we have to make up everything ourselves."

" But who will ever wear such a number of things?
There are only two of you? "

" Oh . . . as though we were thinking of wearing them! They are not to be worn; they are for
the trousseau! "

" Ah, *mamam*, what are you saying? " said the
daughter, and she crimsoned again. " Our visitor
might suppose it was true. I don't intend to be married. Never! "

She said this, but at the very word " married "
her eyes glowed.

Tea, biscuits, butter, and jam were brought in,
followed by raspberries and cream. At seven
o'clock, we had supper, consisting of six courses,
and while we were at supper I heard a loud yawn
from the next room. I looked with surprise towards the door: it was a yawn that could only come
from a man.

" That's my husband's brother, Yegor Semyonitch," the little lady explained, noticing my surprise. " He's been living with us for the last year.
Please excuse him; he cannot come in to see you.
He is such an unsociable person, he is shy with
strangers. He is going into a monastery. He was
unfairly treated in the service, and the disappointment has preyed on his mind."

After supper the little lady showed the vestment
which Yegor Semyonitch was embroidering with his
own hands as an offering for the Church. Manetchka threw off her shyness for a moment and

showed me the tobacco-pouch she was embroidering
for her father.   When I pretended to be greatly
struck by her work, she flushed crimson and whispered something in her mother's ear.   The latter
beamed all over, and invited me to go with her to the
store-room.   There I was shown five large trunks,
and a number of smaller trunks and boxes.

"This is her trousseau," her mother whispered;
"we made it all ourselves."

After looking at these forbidding trunks I took
leave of my hospitable hostesses.   They made me
promise to come and see them again some day.

It happened that I was able to keep this promise.
Seven years after my first visit, I was sent down
to the little town to give expert evidence in a case
that was being tried there.

As I entered the little house I heard the same
"Ach!" echo through it.   They recognised me at
once. . . . Well they might!   My first visit had
been an event in their lives, and when events are few
they are long remembered.

I walked into the drawing-room: the mother, who
had grown stouter and was already getting grey,
was creeping about on the floor, cutting out some
blue material.   The daughter was sitting on the sofa,
embroidering.

There was the same smell of moth powder; there
were the same patterns, the same portrait with the
broken glass.   But yet there was a change.   Beside
the portrait of the bishop hung a portrait of the

Colonel, and the ladies were in mourning. The Colonel's death had occurred a week after his promotion to be a general.

Reminiscences began. . . . The widow shed tears.

"We have had a terrible loss," she said. "My husband, you know, is dead. We are alone in the world now, and have no one but ourselves to look to. Yegor Semyonitch is alive, but I have no good news to tell of him. They would not have him in the monastery on account of — of intoxicating beverages. And now in his disappointment he drinks more than ever. I am thinking of going to the Marshal of Nobility to lodge a complaint. Would you believe it, he has more than once broken open the trunks and . . . taken Manetchka's trousseau and given it to beggars. He has taken everything out of two of the trunks! If he goes on like this, my Manetchka will be left without a trousseau at all."

"What are you saying, *mamam?*" said Manetchka, embarrassed. "Our visitor might suppose . . . there's no knowing what he might suppose. . . . I shall never — never marry."

Manetchka cast her eyes up to the ceiling with a look of hope and aspiration, evidently not for a moment believing what she said.

A little bald-headed masculine figure in a brown coat and goloshes instead of boots darted like a mouse across the passage and disappeared. "Yegor Semyonitch, I suppose," I thought.

I looked at the mother and daughter together. They both looked much older and terribly changed. The mother's hair was silvered, but the daughter was so faded and withered that her mother might have been taken for her elder sister, not more than five years her senior.

" I have made up my mind to go to the Marshal," the mother said to me, forgetting she had told me this already. " I mean to make a complaint. Yegor Semyonitch lays his hands on everything we make, and offers it up for the sake of his soul. My Manetchka is left without a trousseau."

Manetchka flushed again, but this time she said nothing.

" We have to make them all over again. And God knows we are not so well off. We are all alone in the world now."

" We are alone in the world," repeated Manetchka.

A year ago fate brought me once more to the little house.

Walking into the drawing-room, I saw the old lady. Dressed all in black with heavy crape *pleureuses,* she was sitting on the sofa sewing. Beside her sat the little old man in the brown coat and the goloshes instead of boots. On seeing me, he jumped up and ran out of the room.

In response to my greeting, the old lady smiled and said:

" *Je suis charmée de vous revoir, monsieur.*"

"What are you making?" I asked, a little later.

"It's a blouse. When it's finished I shall take it to the priest's to be put away, or else Yegor Semyonitch would carry it off. I store everything at the priest's now," she added in a whisper.

And looking at the portrait of her daughter which stood before her on the table, she sighed and said:

"We are all alone in the world."

And where was the daughter? Where was Manetchka? I did not ask. I did not dare to ask the old mother dressed in her new deep mourning. And while I was in the room, and when I got up to go, no Manetchka came out to greet me. I did not hear her voice, nor her soft, timid foot-step. . . .

I understood, and my heart was heavy.

1883

THE HELPMATE

THE HELPMATE

" I've asked you not to tidy my table," said Nikolay Yevgrafitch. " There's no finding anything when you've tidied up. Where's the telegram? Where have you thrown it? Be so good as to look for it. It's from Kazan, dated yesterday."

The maid — a pale, very slim girl with an indifferent expression — found several telegrams in the basket under the table, and handed them to the doctor without a word; but all these were telegrams from patients. Then they looked in the drawing-room, and in Olga Dmitrievna's room.

It was past midnight. Nikolay Yevgrafitch knew his wife would not be home very soon, not till five o'clock at least. He did not trust her, and when she was long away he could not sleep, was worried, and at the same time he despised his wife, and her bed, and her looking-glass, and her boxes of sweets, and the hyacinths, and the lilies of the valley which were sent her every day by some one or other, and which diffused the sickly fragrance of a florist's shop all over the house. On such nights he became petty, ill-humoured, irritable, and he fancied now that it was very necessary for him to have the telegram he had received the day before from his brother, though it contained nothing but Christmas greetings.

On the table of his wife's room under the box of stationery he found a telegram, and glanced at it casually. It was addressed to his wife, care of his mother-in-law, from Monte Carlo, and signed Michel. . . . The doctor did not understand one word of it, as it was in some foreign language, apparently English.

"Who is this Michel? Why Monte Carlo? Why directed care of her mother?"

During the seven years of his married life he had grown used to being suspicious, guessing, catching at clues, and it had several times occurred to him, that his exercise at home had qualified him to become an excellent detective. Going into his study and beginning to reflect, he recalled at once how he had been with his wife in Petersburg a year and a half ago, and had lunched with an old school-fellow, a civil engineer, and how that engineer had introduced to him and his wife a young man of two or three and twenty, called Mihail Ivanovitch, with rather a curious short surname — Riss. Two months later the doctor had seen the young man's photograph in his wife's album, with an inscription in French: " In remembrance of the present and in hope of the future." Later on he had met the young man himself at his mother-in-law's. And that was at the time when his wife had taken to being very often absent and coming home at four or five o'clock in the morning, and was constantly asking him to get her a passport for abroad, which he kept refusing to do; and a continual feud went on in the house which made him feel ashamed to face the servants.

Six months before, his colleagues had decided that he was going into consumption, and advised him to throw up everything and go to the Crimea. When she heard of this, Olga Dmitrievna affected to be very much alarmed; she began to be affectionate to her husband, and kept assuring him that it would be cold and dull in the Crimea, and that he had much better go to Nice, and that she would go with him, and there would nurse him, look after him, take care of him.

Now, he understood why his wife was so particularly anxious to go to Nice: her Michel lived at Monte Carlo.

He took an English dictionary, and translating the words, and guessing their meaning, by degrees he put together the following sentence: " I drink to the health of my beloved darling, and kiss her little foot a thousand times, and am impatiently expecting her arrival." He pictured the pitiable, ludicrous part he would play if he had agreed to go to Nice with his wife. He felt so mortified that he almost shed tears and began pacing to and fro through all the rooms of the flat in great agitation. His pride, his plebeian fastidiousness, was revolted. Clenching his fists and scowling with disgust, he wondered how he, the son of a village priest, brought up in a clerical school, a plain, straightforward man, a surgeon by profession — how could he have let himself be enslaved, have sunk into such shameful bondage to this weak, worthless, mercenary, low creature.

" ' Little foot ' ! " he muttered to himself, crumpling up the telegram; " ' little foot ' ! "

Of the time when he fell in love and proposed to her, and the seven years that he had been living with her, all that remained in his memory was her long, fragrant hair, a mass of soft lace, and her little feet, which certainly were very small, beautiful feet; and even now it seemed as though he still had from those old embraces the feeling of lace and silk upon his hands and face — and nothing more. Nothing more — that is, not counting hysterics, shrieks, reproaches, threats, and lies — brazen, treacherous lies. He remembered how in his father's house in the village a bird would sometimes chance to fly in from the open air into the house and would struggle desperately against the windowpanes and upset things; so this woman from a class utterly alien to him had flown into his life and made complete havoc of it. The best years of his life had been spent as though in hell, his hopes for happiness shattered and turned into a mockery, his health gone, his rooms as vulgar in their atmosphere as a cocotte's, and of the ten thousand he earned every year he could never save ten roubles to send his old mother in the village, and his debts were already about fifteen thousand. It seemed that if a band of brigands had been living in his rooms his life would not have been so hopelessly, so irremediably ruined as by the presence of this woman.

He began coughing and gasping for breath. He ought to have gone to bed and got warm, but he could not. He kept walking about the rooms, or sat down to the table, nervously fidgeting with a pencil and scribbling mechanically on a paper.

" Trying a pen. . . . A little foot."

By five o'clock he grew weaker and threw all the blame on himself. It seemed to him now that if Olga Dmitrievna had married some one else who might have had a good influence over her — who knows? — she might after all have become a good, straightforward woman. He was a poor psychologist, and knew nothing of the female heart; besides, he was churlish, uninteresting. . . .

" I haven't long to live now," he thought. " I am a dead man, and ought not to stand in the way of the living. It would be strange and stupid to insist upon one's rights now. I'll have it out with her; let her go to the man she loves. . . . I'll give her a divorce. I'll take the blame on myself."

Olga Dmitrievna came in at last, and she walked into the study and sank into a chair just as she was in her white cloak, hat, and overboots.

" The nasty, fat boy," she said with a sob, breath-

ing hard. " It's really dishonest; it's disgusting."
She stamped.   " I can't put up with it; I can't, I
can't ! "

" What's the matter ? " asked Nikolay Yevgrafitch, going up to her.

" That student, Azarbekov, was seeing me home,
and he lost my bag, and there was fifteen roubles in
it.   I borrowed it from mamma."

She was crying in a most genuine way, like a little
girl, and not only her handkerchief, but even her
gloves, were wet with tears.

" It can't be helped ! " said the doctor.   " If he's
lost it, he's lost it, and it's no good worrying over it.
Calm yourself; I want to talk to you."

" I am not a millionaire to lose money like that.
He says he'll pay it back, but I don't believe him;
he's poor . . ."

Her husband begged her to calm herself and to
listen to him, but she kept on talking of the student
and of the fifteen roubles she had lost.

" Ach !   I'll give you twenty-five roubles to-morrow if you'll only hold your tongue ! " he said irritably.

" I must take off my things ! " she said, crying.
" I can't talk seriously in my fur coat !   How
strange you are ! "

He helped her off with her coat and overboots,
detecting as he did so the smell of the white wine
she liked to drink with oysters (in spite of her
etherealness she ate and drank a great deal).   She

went into her room and came back soon after, having changed her things and powdered her face, though her eyes still showed traces of tears. She sat down, retreating into her light, lacy dressing-gown, and in the mass of billowy pink her husband could see nothing but her hair, which she had let down, and her little foot wearing a slipper.

"What do you want to talk about?" she asked, swinging herself in a rocking-chair.

"I happened to see this;" and he handed her the telegram.

She read it and shrugged her shoulders.

"Well?" she said, rocking herself faster. "That's the usual New Year's greeting and nothing else. There are no secrets in it."

"You are reckoning on my not knowing English. No, I don't know it; but I have a dictionary. That telegram is from Riss; he drinks to the health of his beloved and sends you a thousand kisses. But let us leave that," the doctor went on hurriedly. "I don't in the least want to reproach you or make a scene. We've had scenes and reproaches enough; it's time to make an end of them. . . . This is what I want to say to you: you are free, and can live as you like."

There was a silence. She began crying quietly.

"I set you free from the necessity of lying and keeping up pretences," Nikolay Yevgrafitch continued. "If you love that young man, love him; if you want to go abroad to him, go. You are young, healthy, and I am a wreck, and haven't long to live. In short . . . you understand me."

He was agitated and could not go on.   Olga Dmitrievna, crying and speaking in a voice of self-pity, acknowledged that she loved Riss, and used to drive out of town with him and see him in his rooms, and now she really did long to go abroad.

" You see, I hide nothing from you," she added, with a sigh.   " My whole soul lies open before you. And I beg you again, be generous, get me a passport."

" I repeat, you are free."

She moved to another seat nearer him to look at the expression of his face.   She did not believe him and wanted now to understand his secret meaning. She never did believe any one, and however generous were their intentions, she always suspected some petty or ignoble motive or selfish object in them.   And when she looked searchingly into his face, it seemed to him that there was a gleam of green light in her eyes as in a cat's.

" When shall I get the passport? " she asked softly.

He suddenly had an impulse to say " Never "; but he restrained himself and said:

" When you like."

" I shall only go for a month."

" You'll go to Riss for good.   I'll get you a divorce, take the blame on myself, and Riss can marry you."

"But I don't want a divorce!" Olga Dmitrievna retorted quickly, with an astonished face. "I am not asking you for a divorce! Get me a passport, that's all."

"But why don't you want the divorce?" asked the doctor, beginning to feel irritated. "You are a strange woman. How strange you are! If you are fond of him in earnest and he loves you too, in your position you can do nothing better than get married. Can you really hesitate between marriage and adultery?"

"I understand you," she said, walking away from him, and a spiteful, vindictive expression came into her face. "I understand you perfectly. You are sick of me, and you simply want to get rid of me, to force this divorce on me. Thank you very much; I am not such a fool as you think. I won't accept the divorce and I won't leave you — I won't, I won't! To begin with, I don't want to lose my position in society," she continued quickly, as though afraid of being prevented from speaking. "Secondly, I am twenty-seven and Riss is only twenty-three; he'll be tired of me in a year and throw me over. And what's more, if you care to know, I'm not certain that my feeling will last long . . . so there! I'm not going to leave you."

"Then I'll turn you out of the house!" shouted Nikolay Yevgrafitch, stamping. "I shall turn you out, you vile, loathsome woman!"

"We shall see!" she said, and went out.

It was broad daylight outside, but the doctor still sat at the table moving the pencil over the paper and writing mechanically.

" My dear Sir. . . . Little foot."

Or he walked about and stopped in the drawing-room before a photograph taken seven years ago, soon after his marriage, and looked at it for a long time.   It was a family group: his father-in-law, his mother-in-law, his wife Olga Dmitrievna when she was twenty, and himself in the rôle of a happy young husband.   His father-in-law, a clean-shaven, drop-sical privy councillor, crafty and avaricious; his mother-in-law, a stout lady with small predatory features like a weasel, who loved her daughter to distraction and helped her in everything; if her daughter were strangling some one, the mother would not have protested, but would only have screened her with her skirts.   Olga Dmitrievna, too, had small predatory-looking features, but more expressive and bolder than her mother's; she was not a weasel, but a beast on a bigger scale!   And Nikolay Yevgrafitch himself in the photograph looked such a guileless soul, such a kindly, good fel-low, so open and simple-hearted; his whole face was relaxed in the naïve, good-natured smile of a divin-ity student, and he had had the simplicity to be-lieve that that company of beasts of prey into which destiny had chanced to thrust him would give him romance and happiness and all he had dreamed of when as a student he used to sing the song " Youth is wasted, life is nought, when the heart is cold and loveless."

And once more he asked himself in perplexity how he, the son of a village priest, with his democratic bringing up — a plain, blunt, straightforward man — could have so helplessly surrendered to the power of this worthless, false, vulgar, petty creature, whose nature was so utterly alien to him.

When at eleven o'clock he put on his coat to go to the hospital the servant came into his study.

"What is it?" he asked.

"The mistress has got up and asks you for the twenty-five roubles you promised her yesterday."

1892

TALENT

TALENT

AN artist called Yegor Savvitch, who was spending
his summer holidays at the house of an officer's
widow, was sitting on his bed, given up to the depression of morning. It was beginning to look like
autumn out of doors. Heavy, clumsy clouds covered the sky in thick layers; there was a cold, pierc-
ing wind, and with a plaintive wail the trees were all
bending on one side. He could see the yellow leaves
whirling round in the air and on the earth. Fare-
well, summer! This melancholy of nature is beautiful and poetical in its own way, when it is looked
at with the eyes of an artist, but Yegor Savvitch
was in no humour to see beauty. He was devoured
by ennui and his only consolation was the thought
that by to-morrow he would not be there. The bed,
the chairs, the tables, the floor, were all heaped up
with cushions, crumpled bed-clothes, boxes. The
floor had not been swept, the cotton curtains had
been taken down from the windows. Next day he
was moving to town.

His landlady, the widow, was out. She had
gone off somewhere to hire horses and carts to move
next day to town. Profiting by the absence of her
severe mamma, her daughter Katya, aged twenty,
had for a long time been sitting in the young man's

room. Next day the painter was going away, and she had a great deal to say to him. She kept talking, talking, and yet she felt that she had not said a tenth of what she wanted to say. With her eyes full of tears, she gazed at his shaggy head, gazed at it with rapture and sadness. And Yegor Savvitch was shaggy to a hideous extent, so that he looked like a wild animal. His hair hung down to his shoulder-blades, his beard grew from his neck, from his nostrils, from his ears; his eyes were lost under his thick overhanging brows. It was all so thick, so matted, that if a fly or a beetle had been caught in his hair, it would never have found its way out of this enchanted thicket. Yegor Savvitch listened to Katya, yawning. He was tired. When Katya began whimpering, he looked severely at her from his overhanging eyebrows, frowned, and said in a heavy, deep bass:

" I cannot marry."

" Why not? " Katya asked softly.

" Because for a painter, and in fact any man who lives for art, marriage is out of the question. An artist must be free."

" But in what way should I hinder you, Yegor Savvitch? "

" I am not speaking of myself, I am speaking in general. . . . Famous authors and painters have never married."

" And you, too, will be famous — I understand that perfectly. But put yourself in my place. I am afraid of my mother. She is stern and irritable. When she knows that you won't marry me, and that it's all nothing . . . she'll begin to give it to me. Oh, how wretched I am! And you haven't paid for your rooms, either! . . ."

"Damn her! I'll pay."

Yegor Savvitch got up and began walking to and fro.

"I ought to be abroad!" he said. And the artist told her that nothing was easier than to go abroad. One need do nothing but paint a picture and sell it.

"Of course!" Katya assented. "Why haven't you painted one in the summer?"

"Do you suppose I can work in a barn like this?" the artist said ill-humouredly. "And where should I get models?"

Some one banged the door viciously in the storey below. Katya, who was expecting her mother's return from minute to minute, jumped up and ran away. The artist was left alone. For a long time he walked to and fro, threading his way between the chairs and the piles of untidy objects of all sorts. He heard the widow rattling the crockery and loudly abusing the peasants who had asked her two roubles for each cart. In his disgust Yegor Savvitch stopped before the cupboard and stared for a long while, frowning at the decanter of vodka.

"Ah, blast you!" he heard the widow railing at Katya. "Damnation take you!"

The artist drank a glass of vodka, and the dark cloud in his soul gradually disappeared, and he felt as though all his inside was smiling within him. He began dreaming. . . . His fancy pictured how he would become great. He could not imagine his future works but he could see distinctly how the papers would talk of him, how the shops would sell his photographs, with what envy his friends would look after him. He tried to picture himself in a magnificent drawing-room surrounded by pretty and adoring women; but the picture was misty, vague, as he had never in his life seen a drawing-room. The pretty and adoring women were not a success either, for, except Katya, he knew no adoring woman, not even one respectable girl. People who know nothing about life usually picture life from books, but Yegor Savvitch knew no books either. He had tried to read Gogol, but had fallen asleep on the second page.

"It won't burn, drat the thing!" the widow bawled down below, as she set the samovar. "Katya, give me some charcoal!"

The dreamy artist felt a longing to share his hopes and dreams with some one. He went downstairs into the kitchen, where the stout widow and Katya were busy about a dirty stove in the midst of charcoal fumes from the samovar. There he sat down on a bench close to a big pot and began:

"It's a fine thing to be an artist! I can go just where I like, do what I like. One has not to work in an office or in the fields. I've no superiors or officers over me. . . . I'm my own superior. And with all that I'm doing good to humanity!"

And after dinner he composed himself for a "rest." He usually slept till the twilight of evening. But this time soon after dinner he felt that some one was pulling at his leg. Some one kept laughing and shouting his name. He opened his eyes and saw his friend Ukleikin, the landscape painter, who had been away all the summer in the Kostroma district.

"Bah!" he cried, delighted. "What do I see?"

There followed handshakes, questions.

"Well, have you brought anything? I suppose you've knocked off hundreds of sketches?" said Yegor Savvitch, wathing Ukleikin taking his belongings out of his trunk.

"H'm! . . . Yes. I have done something. And how are you getting on? Have you been painting anything?"

Yegor Savvitch dived behind the bed, and crimson in the face, extracted a canvas in a frame covered with dust and spider webs.

"See here. . . . A girl at the window after parting from her betrothed. In three sittings. Not neary finished yet."

The picture represented Katya faintly outlined sitting at an open window, from which could be seen a garden and lilac distance. Ukleikin did not like the picture.

" H'm! . . . There is air and . . . and there is expression," he said. " There's a feeling of distance, but . . . but that bush is screaming . . . screaming horribly! "

The decanter was brought on to the scene.

Towards evening Kostyliov, also a promising beginner, an historical painter, came in to see Yegor Savvitch. He was a friend staying at the next villa, and was a man of five-and-thirty. He had long hair, and wore a blouse with a Shakespeare collar, and had a dignified manner. Seeing the vodka, he frowned, complained of his chest, but yielding to his friends' entreaties, drank a glass.

" I've thought of a subject, my friends," he began, getting drunk. " I want to paint some new . . . Herod or Clepentian, or some blackguard of that description, you understand, and to contrast with him the idea of Christianity. On the one side Rome, you understand, and on the other Christianity. . . . I want to represent the spirit, you understand? The spirit! "

And the widow downstairs shouted continually:

" Katya, give me the cucumbers! Go to Sidorov's and get some kvass, you jade! "

Like wolves in a cage, the three friends kept pacing to and fro from one end of the room to the other. They talked without ceasing, talked, hotly and genuinely; all three were excited, carried away. To listen to them it would seem they had the future, fame, money, in their hands. And it never occurred to either of them that time was passing, that every day life was nearing its close, that they had lived at other people's expense a great deal and nothing yet was accomplished; that they were all bound by the inexorable law by which of a hundred promising beginners only two or three rise to any position and all the others draw blanks in the lottery, perish playing the part of flesh for the cannon. . . . They were gay and happy, and looked the future boldly in the face!

At one o'clock in the morning Kostyliov said good-bye, and smoothing out his Shakespeare collar, went home. The landscape painter remained to sleep at Yegor Savvitch's. Before going to bed, Yegor Savvitch took a candle and made his way into the kitchen to get a drink of water. In the dark, narrow passage Katya was sitting, on a box, and, with her hands clasped on her knees, was looking upwards. A blissful smile was straying on her pale, exhausted face, and her eyes were beaming.

" Is that you? What are you thinking about? " Yegor Savvitch asked her.

" I am thinking of how you'll be famous," she said in a half-whisper. " I keep fancying how you'll become a famous man. . . . I overheard all your talk. . . . I keep dreaming and dreaming. . . ."

Katya went off into a happy laugh, cried, and laid her hands reverently on her idol's shoulders.

1886

AN ARTIST'S STORY

AN ARTIST'S STORY

I

It was six or seven years ago when I was living in one of the districts of the province of T——, on the estate of a young landowner called Byelokurov, who used to get up very early, wear a peasant tunic, drink beer in the evenings, and continually complain to me that he never met with sympathy from any one. He lived in the lodge in the garden, and I in the old seigniorial house, in a big room with columns, where there was no furniture except a wide sofa on which I used to sleep, and a table on which I used to lay out patience. There was always, even in still weather, a droning noise in the old Amos stoves, and in thunder-storms the whole house shook and seemed to be cracking into pieces; and it was rather terrifying, especially at night, when all the ten big windows were suddenly lit up by lightning.

Condemned by destiny to perpetual idleness, I did absolutely nothing. For hours together I gazed out of window at the sky, at the birds, at the avenue, read everything that was brought me by post, slept. Sometimes I went out of the house and wandered about till late in the evening.

One day as I was returning home, I accidentally

strayed into a place I did not know.   The sun was already sinking, and the shades of evening lay across the flowering rye.   Two rows of old, closely planted, very tall fir-trees stood like two dense walls forming a picturesque, gloomy avenue.   I easily climbed over the fence and walked along the avenue, slipping over the fir-needles which lay two inches deep on the ground.   It was still and dark, and only here and there on the high tree-tops the vivid golden light quivered and made rainbows in the spiders' webs.   There was a strong, almost stifling smell of resin.   Then I turned into a long avenue of limes. Here, too, all was desolation and age; last year's leaves rusted mournfully under my feet and in the twilight shadows lurked between the trees.   From the old orchard on the right came the faint, reluctant note of the golden oriole, who must have been old too.   But at last the limes ended.   I walked by an old white house of two storeys with a terrace, and there suddenly opened before me a view of a courtyard, a large pond with a bathing-house, a group of green willows, and a village on the further bank, with a high, narrow belfry on which there glittered a cross reflecting the setting sun.

For a moment it breathed upon me the fascination of something near and very familiar, as though I had seen that landscape at some time in my childhood.

At the white stone gates which led from the yard to the fields, old-fashioned solid gates with lions on them, were standing two girls. One of them, the elder, a slim, pale, very handsome girl with a perfect haystack of chestnut hair and a little obstinate mouth, had a severe expression and scarcely took notice of me, while the other, who was still very young, not more than seventeen or eighteen, and was also slim and pale, with a large mouth and large eyes, looked at me with astonishment as I passed by, said something in English, and was overcome with embarrassment. And it seemed to me that these two charming faces, too, had long been familiar to me. And I returned home feeling as though I had had a delightful dream.

One morning soon afterwards, as Byelokurov and I were walking near the house, a carriage drove unexpectedly into the yard, rustling over the grass, and in it was sitting one of those girls. It was the elder one. She had come to ask for subscriptions for some villagers whose cottages had been burnt down. Speaking with great earnestness and precision, and not looking at us, she told us how many houses in the village of Siyanovo had been burnt, how many men, women, and children were left homeless, and what steps were proposed, to begin with, by the Relief Committee, of which she was now a member. After handing us the subscription list for our signatures, she put it away and immediately began to take leave of us.

"You have quite forgotten us, Pyotr Petrovitch," she said to Byelokurov as she shook hands with

him. " Do come, and if Monsieur N. (she mentioned my name) cares to make the acquaintance of
admirers of his work, and will come and see us,
mother and I will be delighted."

I bowed.

When she had gone Pyotr Petrovitch began to
tell me about her.   The girl was, he said, of good
family, and her name was Lidia Voltchaninov, and
the estate on which she lived with her mother and
sister, like the village on the other side of the pond,
was called Shelkovka.   Her father had once held
an important position in Moscow, and had died with
the rank of privy councillor.   Although they had
ample means, the Voltchaninovs lived on their estate summer and winter without going away.   Lidia
was a teacher in the Zemstvo school in her own village, and received a salary of twenty-five roubles
a month.   She spent nothing on herself but her salary, and was proud of earning her own living.

    " An   interesting   family,"   said   Byelokurov.
" Let us go over one day.   They will be delighted to
see you."

    One afternoon on a holiday we thought of the
Voltchaninovs, and went to Shelkovka to see them.
They — the mother and two daughters — were at
home.   The mother, Ekaterina Pavlovna, who at
one time had been handsome, but now, asthmatic,
depressed, vague, and over-feeble for her years,
tried to entertain me with conversation about painting.   Having heard from her daughter that I might

come to Shelkovka, she had hurriedly recalled two
or three of my landscapes which she had seen in exhibitions in Moscow, and now asked what I meant
to express by them. Lidia, or as they called her
Lida, talked more to Byelokurov than to me.
Earnest and unsmiling, she asked him why he was
not on the Zemstvo, and why he had not attended
any of its meetings.

"It's not right, Pyotr Petrovitch," she said reproachfully. "It's not right. It's too bad."

"That's true, Lida — that's true," the mother assented. "It isn't right."

"Our whole district is in the hands of Balagin,"
Lida went on, addressing me. "He is the chairman of the Zemstvo Board, and he has distributed
all the posts in the district among his nephews and
sons-in-law; and he does as he likes. He ought to
be opposed. The young men ought to make a
strong party, but you see what the young men among
us are like. It's a shame, Pyotr Petrovitch!"

The younger sister, Genya, was silent while they
were talking of the Zemstvo. She took no part in
serious conversation. She was not looked upon as
quite grown up by her family, and, like a child, was
always called by the nickname of Misuce, because
that was what she had called her English governess
when she was a child. She was all the time looking at me with curiosity, and when I glanced at the
photographs in the album, she explained to me:
"That's uncle . . . that's god-father," moving her

finger across the photograph.   As she did so she
touched me with her shoulder like a child, and I had
a close view of her delicate, undeveloped chest, her
slender shoulders, her plait, and her thin little body
tightly drawn in by her sash.

We played croquet and lawn tennis, we walked
about the garden, drank tea, and then sat a long
time over supper.   After the huge empty room with
columns, I felt, as it were, at home in this small
snug house where there were no oleographs on the
walls and where the servants were spoken to with
civility.   And everything seemed to me young and
pure, thanks to the presence of Lida and Misuce,
and there was an atmosphere of refinement over
everything.   At supper Lida talked to Byelokurov
again of the Zemstvo, of Balagin, and of school
libraries.   She was an energetic, genuine girl, with
convictions, and it was interesting to listen to her,
though she talked a great deal and in a loud voice
— perhaps because she was accustomed to talking
at school.   On the other hand, Pyotr Petrovitch,
who had retained from his student days the habit
of turning every conversation into an argument, was
tedious, flat, long-winded, and unmistakably anxious
to appear clever and advanced.   Gesticulating, he
upset a sauce-boat with his sleeve, making a huge
pool on the tablecloth, but no one except me appeared to notice it.

It was dark and still as we went home.

" Good breeding is shown, not by not upsetting

the sauce, but by not noticing it when somebody else does," said Byelokurov, with a sigh. "Yes, a splendid, intellectual family! I've dropped out of all decent society; it's dreadful how I've dropped out of it! It's all through work, work, work!"

He talked of how hard one had to work if one wanted to be a model farmer. And I thought what a heavy, sluggish fellow he was! Whenever he talked of anything serious he articulated " Er-er " with intense effort, and worked just as he talked — slowly, always late and behind-hand. I had little faith in his business capacity if only from the fact that when I gave him letters to post he carried them about in his pocket for weeks together.

"The hardest thing of all," he muttered as he walked beside me —" the hardest thing of all is that, work as one may, one meets with no sympathy from any one. No sympathy!"

II

I took to going to see the Voltchaninovs. As a rule I sat on the lower step of the terrace; I was fretted by dissatisfaction with myself; I was sorry at the thought of my life passing so rapidly and un-interestingly, and felt as though I would like to tear out of my breast the heart which had grown so heavy. And meanwhile I heard talk on the terrace, the rustling of dresses, the pages of a book being turned. I soon grew accustomed to the idea that during the day Lida received patients, gave out books, and often went into the village with a parasol and no hat, and in the evening talked aloud of the Zemstvo and schools. This slim, handsome, invariably austere girl, with her small well-cut mouth, always said dryly when the conversation turned on serious subjects:

" That's of no interest to you."

She did not like me. She disliked me because I was a landscape painter and did not in my pictures portray the privations of the peasants, and that, as she fancied, I was indifferent to what she put such faith in. I remember when I was travelling on the banks of Lake Baikal, I met a Buriat girl on horseback, wearing a shirt and trousers of blue Chinese canvas; I asked her if she would sell me her pipe. While we talked she looked contemptuously at my European face and hat, and in a moment she was bored with talking to me; she shouted to her horse and galloped on. And in just the same way Lida despised me as an alien. She never outwardly expressed her dislike for me, but I felt it, and sitting on the lower step of the terrace, I felt irritated, and said that doctoring peasants when one was not a doctor was deceiving them, and that it was easy to be benevolent when one had six thousand acres.

Meanwhile her sister Misuce had no cares, and spent her life in complete idleness just as I did. When she got up in the morning she immediately took up a book and sat down to read on the terrace in a deep arm-chair, with her feet hardly touching the ground, or hid herself with her book in the lime avenue, or walked out into the fields. She spent the whole day reading, poring greedily over her book, and only from the tired, dazed look in her eyes and the extreme paleness of her face one could divine how this continual reading exhausted her brain. When I arrived she would flush a little, leave her book, and looking into my face with her big eyes, would tell me eagerly of anything that had happened — for instance, that the chimney had been on fire in the servants' hall, or that one of the men had caught a huge fish in the pond. On ordinary days she usually went about in a light blouse and a dark blue skirt. We went for walks together, picked cherries for making jam, went out in the boat. When she jumped up to reach a cherry or sculled in the boat, her thin, weak arms showed through her transparent sleeves. Or I painted a sketch, and she stood beside me watching rapturously.

One Sunday at the end of July I came to the Voltchaninovs about nine o'clock in the morning. I walked about the park, keeping a good distance from the house, looking for white mushrooms, of which there was a great number that summer, and noting their position so as to come and pick them afterwards with Genya. There was a warm breeze. I saw Genya and her mother both in light holiday dresses coming home from church, Genya holding her hat in the wind. Afterwards I heard them having tea on the terrace.

For a careless person like me, trying to find justification for my perpetual idleness, these holiday
mornings in our country-houses in the summer have
always had a particular charm. When the green
garden, still wet with dew, is all sparkling in the
sun and looks radiant with happiness, when there
is a scent of mignonette and oleander near the
house, when the young people have just come back
from church and are having breakfast in the garden, all so charmingly dressed and gay, and one
knows that all these healthy, well-fed, handsome people are going to do nothing the whole long day, one
wishes that all life were like that. Now, too, I had
the same thought, and walked about the garden prepared to walk about like that, aimless and unoccu-
pied, the whole day, the whole summer.

Genya came out with a basket; she had a look in
her face as though she knew she would find me in
the garden, or had a presentiment of it. We gathered mushrooms and talked, and when she asked
a question she walked a little ahead so as to see my
face.

" A miracle happened in the village yesterday,"
she said. " The lame woman Pelagea has been ill
the whole year. No doctors or medicines did her
any good; but yesterday an old woman came and
whispered something over her, and her illness passed
away."

" That's nothing much," I said. " You mustn't

look for miracles only among sick people and old women. Isn't health a miracle? And life itself? Whatever is beyond understanding is a miracle."

" And aren't you afraid of what is beyond understanding? "

" No. Phenomena I don't understand I face boldly, and am not overwhelmed by them. I am above them. Man ought to recognise himself as superior to lions, tigers, stars, superior to everything in nature, even what seems miraculous and is beyond his understanding, or else he is not a man, but a mouse afraid of everything."

Genya believed that as an artist I knew a very great deal, and could guess correctly what I did not know. She longed for me to initiate her into the domain of the Eternal and the Beautiful — into that higher world in which, as she imagined, I was quite at home. And she talked to me of God, of the eternal life, of the miraculous. And I, who could never admit that my self and my imagination would be lost forever after death, answered: " Yes, men are immortal "; " Yes, there is eternal life in store for us." And she listened, believed, and did not ask for proofs.

As we were going home she stopped suddenly and said:

" Our Lida is a remarkable person — isn't she? I love her very dearly, and would be ready to give my life for her any minute. But tell me "— Genya

touched my sleeve with her finger —" tell me, why
do you always argue with her? Why are you irritated?"

" Because she is wrong."

Genya shook her head and tears came into her
eyes.

" How incomprehensible that is! " she said.

At that minute Lida had just returned from
somewhere, and standing with a whip in her hand,
a slim, beautiful figure in the sunlight, at the steps,
she was giving some orders to one of the men.
Talking loudly, she hurriedly received two or three
sick villagers; then with a busy and anxious face she
walked about the rooms, opening one cupboard after
another, and went upstairs. It was a long time
before they could find her and call her to dinner,
and she came in when we had finished our soup.
All these tiny details I remember with tenderness,
and that whole day I remember vividly, though nothing special happened. After dinner Genya lay in
a long arm-chair reading, while I sat upon the bottom step of the terrace. We were silent. The
whole sky was overcast with clouds, and it began to
spot with fine rain. It was hot; the wind had
dropped, and it seemed as though the day would
never end. Ekaterina Pavlovna came out on the
terrace, looking drowsy and carrying a fan.

" Oh, mother," said Genya, kissing her hand,
" it's not good for you to sleep in the day."

They adored each other. When one went into

the garden, the other would stand on the terrace, and, looking towards the trees, call " Aa — oo, Genya!" or " Mother, where are you?" They always said their prayers together, and had the same faith; and they understood each other perfectly even when they did not speak. And their attitude to people was the same. Ekaterina Pavlovna, too, grew quickly used to me and fond of me, and when I did not come for two or three days, sent to ask if I were well. She, too, gazed at my sketches with enthusiasm, and with the same openness and readiness to chatter as Misuce, she told me what had happened, and confided to me her domestic secrets.

She had a perfect reverence for her elder daughter. Lida did not care for endearments, she talked only of serious matters; she lived her life apart, and to her mother and sister was as sacred and enigmatic a person as the admiral, always sitting in his cabin, is to the sailors.

" Our Lida is a remarkable person," the mother would often say. " Isn't she?"

Now, too, while it was drizzling with rain, we talked of Lida.

" She is a remarkable girl," said her mother, and added in an undertone, like a conspirator, looking about her timidly: " You wouldn't easily find another like her; only, do you know, I am beginning to be a little uneasy. The school, the dispensary, books — all that's very good, but why go to extremes? She is three-and-twenty, you know; it's time for her to think seriously of herself. With her books and her dispensary she will find life has slipped by without having noticed it. . . . She must be married."

Genya, pale from reading, with her hair disarranged, raised her head and said as it were to herself, looking at her mother:

" Mother, everything is in God's hands."

And again she buried herself in her book.

Byelokurov came in his tunic and embroidered shirt. We played croquet and tennis, then when it got dark, sat a long time over supper and talked again about schools, and about Balagin, who had the whole district under his thumb. As I went away from the Voltchaninovs that evening, I carried away the impression of a long, long idle day, with a melancholy consciousness that everything ends in this world, however long it may be.

Genya saw us out to the gate, and perhaps because she had been with me all day, from morning till night, I felt dull without her, and that all that charming family were near and dear to me, and for the first time that summer I had a yearning to paint.

" Tell me, why do you lead such a dreary, colourless life? " I asked Byelokurov as I went home. " My life is dreary, difficult, and monotonous because I am an artist, a strange person. From my earliest days I've been wrung by envy, self-dissatisfaction, distrust in my work. I'm always poor, I'm a wanderer, but you — you're a healthy, normal

man, a landowner, and a gentleman. Why do you
live in such an uninteresting way? Why do you get
so little out of life? Why haven't you, for instance,
fallen in love with Lida or Genya?"

"You forget that I love another woman," answered Byelokurov.

He was referring to Liubov Ivanovna, the lady
who shared the lodge with him. Every day I saw
this lady, very plump, rotund, and dignified, not unlike a fat goose, walking about the garden, in the
Russian national dress and beads, always carrying
a parasol; and the servant was continually calling
her in to dinner or to tea. Three years before she
had taken one of the lodges for a summer holiday,
and had settled down at Byelokurov's apparently
forever. She was ten years older than he was, and
kept a sharp hand over him, so much so that he
had to ask her permission when he went out of the
house. She often sobbed in a deep masculine note,
and then I used to send word to her that if she did
not leave off, I should give up my rooms there; and
she left off.

When we got home Byelokurov sat down on the
sofa and frowned thoughtfully, and I began walking up and down the room, conscious of a soft emotion as though I were in love. I wanted to talk
about the Voltchaninovs.

"Lida could only fall in love with a member of
the Zemstvo, as devoted to schools and hospitals as
she is," I said. "Oh, for the sake of a girl like that

one might not only go into the Zemstvo, but even wear out iron shoes, like the girl in the fairy tale. And Misuce? What a sweet creature she is, that Misuce!"

Byelokurov, drawling out "Er — er," began a long-winded disquisition on the malady of the age — pessimism. He talked confidently, in a tone that suggested that I was opposing him. Hundreds of miles of desolate, monotonous, burnt-up steppe cannot induce such deep depression as one man when he sits and talks, and one does not know when he will go.

"It's not a question of pessimism or optimism," I said irritably; "it's simply that ninety-nine people out of a hundred have no sense."

Byelokurov took this as aimed at himself, was offended, and went away.

III

"The prince is staying at Malozyomovo, and he asks to be remembered to you," said Lida to her mother. She had just come in, and was taking off her gloves. "He gave me a great deal of interesting news. . . . He promised to raise the question of a medical relief centre at Malozyomovo again at the provincial assembly, but he says there is very little hope of it." And turning to me, she said: "Excuse me, I always forget that this cannot be interesting to you."

I felt irritated.

"Why not interesting to me?" I said, shrugging my shoulders. "You do not care to know my opinion, but I assure you the question has great interest for me."

"Yes?"

"Yes. In my opinion a medical relief centre at Malozyomovo is quite unnecessary."

My irritation infected her; she looked at me, screwing up her eyes, and asked:

"What is necessary? Landscapes?"

"Landscapes are not, either. Nothing is."

She finished taking off her gloves, and opened the newspaper, which had just been brought from the post. A minute later she said quietly, evidently restraining herself:

"Last week Anna died in childbirth, and if there had been a medical relief centre near, she would have lived. And I think even landscape-painters ought to have some opinions on the subject."

"I have a very definite opinion on that subject, I assure you," I answered; and she screened herself with the newspaper, as though unwilling to listen to me. "To my mind, all these schools, dispensaries, libraries, medical relief centres, under present conditions, only serve to aggravate the bondage of the people. The peasants are fettered by a great chain, and you do not break the chain, but only add fresh links to it — that's my view of it."

She raised her eyes to me and smiled ironically, and I went on trying to formulate my leading idea.

"What matters is not that Anna died in child-birth, but that all these Annas, Mavras, Pelageas, toil from early morning till dark, fall ill from working beyond their strength, all their lives tremble for their sick and hungry children, all their lives are being doctored, and in dread of death and disease, fade and grow old early, and die in filth and stench. Their children begin the same story over again as soon as they grow up, and so it goes on for hundreds of years and milliards of men live worse than beasts — in continual terror, for a mere crust of bread. The whole horror of their position lies in their never having time to think of their souls, of their image and semblance. Cold, hunger, animal terror, a burden of toil, like avalanches of snow, block for them every way to spiritual activity — that is, to what distinguishes man from the brutes and what is the only thing which makes life worth living. You go to their help with hospitals and schools, but you don't free them from their fetters by that; on the contrary, you bind them in closer bonds, as, by introducing new prejudices, you increase the number of their wants, to say nothing of the fact that they've got to pay the Zemstvo for blisters and books, and so toil harder than ever."

"I am not going to argue with you," said Lida, putting down the paper. "I've heard all that before. I will only say one thing: one cannot sit with one's hands in one's lap. It's true that we are not saving humanity, and perhaps we make a great many

mistakes; but we do what we can, and we are right.
The highest and holiest task for a civilised being
is to serve his neighbours, and we try to serve them
as best we can. You don't like it, but one can't
please every one."

"That's true, Lida," said her mother —"that's
true."

In Lida's presence she was always a little timid,
and looked at her nervously as she talked, afraid
of saying something superfluous or inopportune.
And she never contradicted her, but always assented:
"That's true, Lida — that's true."

"Teaching the peasants to read and write, books
of wretched precepts and rhymes, and medical relief centres, cannot diminish either ignorance or the
death-rate, just as the light from your windows cannot light up this huge garden," said I. "You give
nothing. By meddling in these people's lives you
only create new wants in them, and new demands
on their labour."

"Ach! Good heavens! But one must do something!" said Lida with vexation, and from her tone
one could see that she thought my arguments worthless and despised them.

"The people must be freed from hard physical
labour," said I. "We must lighten their yoke, let
them have time to breathe, that they may not spend
all their lives at the stove, at the wash-tub, and in
the fields, but may also have time to think of their
souls, of God — may have time to develop their

spiritual capacities.   The highest vocation of man is spiritual activity — the perpetual search for truth and the meaning of life.   Make coarse animal labour unnecessary for them, let them feel themselves free, and then you will see what a mockery these dispensaries and books are.   Once a man recognises his true vocation, he can only be satisfied by religion, science, and art, and not by these trifles."

" Free them from labour ? " laughed Lida.   " But is that possible ? "

" Yes.   Take upon yourself a share of their labour.   If all of us, townspeople and country people, all without exception, would agree to divide between us the labour which mankind spends on the satisfaction of their physical needs, each of us would perhaps need to work only for two or three hours a day.   Imagine that we all, rich and poor, work only for three hours a day, and the rest of our time is free.   Imagine further that in order to depend even less upon our bodies and to labour less, we invent machines to replace our work, we try to cut down our needs to the minimum.   We would harden ourselves and our children that they should not be afraid of hunger and cold, and that we shouldn't be continually trembling for their health like Anna, Mavra, and Pelagea.   Imagine that we don't doctor ourselves, don't keep dispensaries, tobacco factories, distilleries — what a lot of free time would be left us after all!   All of us together would devote our leisure to science and art.   Just as the peasants sometimes work, the whole community together mending the roads, so all of us, as a community, would search for truth and the meaning of life, and I am convinced that the truth would be discovered very quickly; man would escape from this continual, agonising, oppressive dread of death, and even from death itself."

"You contradict yourself, though," said Lida. "You talk about science, and are yourself opposed to elementary education."

"Elementary education when a man has nothing to read but the signs on public houses and sometimes books which he cannot understand — such education has existed among us since the times of Rurik; Gogol's Petrushka has been reading for ever so long, yet as the village was in the days of Rurik so it has remained. What is needed is not elementary education, but freedom for a wide development of spiritual capacities. What are wanted are not schools, but universities."

"You are opposed to medicine, too."

"Yes. It would be necessary only for the study of diseases as natural phenomena, and not for the cure of them. If one must cure, it should not be diseases, but the causes of them. Remove the principal cause — physical labour, and then there will be no disease. I don't believe in a science that cures disease," I went on excitedly. "When science and art are real, they aim not at temporary private ends, but at eternal and universal — they seek for truth and the meaning of life, they seek for God, for the soul, and when they are tied down to the needs and evils of the day, to dispensaries and libraries, they only complicate and hamper life. We have plenty of doctors, chemists, lawyers, plenty of people can read and write, but we are quite without biologists, mathematicians, philosophers, poets. The whole of our intelligence, the whole of our spiritual energy, is spent on satisfying temporary, passing needs. Scientific men, writers, artists, are hard at work; thanks to them, the conveniences of life are multiplied from day to day. Our physical demands increase, yet truth is still a long way off, and man still remains the most rapacious and dirty animal; everything is tending to the degeneration of the majority of mankind, and the loss forever of all fitness for life. In such conditions an artist's work has no meaning, and the more talented he is, the stranger and the more unintelligible is his position, as when one looks into it, it is evident that he is working for the amusement of a rapacious and unclean animal, and is supporting the existing order. And I don't care to work and I won't work. . . . Nothing is any use; let the earth sink to perdition!"

"Misuce, go out of the room!" said Lida to her sister, apparently thinking my words pernicious to the young girl.

Genya looked mournfully at her mother and sister, and went out of the room.

"These are the charming things people say when

they want to justify their indifference," said Lida. "It is easier to disapprove of schools and hospitals, than to teach or heal."

"That's true, Lida — that's true," the mother assented.

"You threaten to give up working," said Lida. "You evidently set a high value on your work. Let us give up arguing; we shall never agree, since I put the most imperfect dispensary or library of which you have just spoken so contemptuously on a higher level than any landscape." And turning at once to her mother, she began speaking in quite a different tone: "The prince is very much changed, and much thinner than when he was with us last. He is being sent to Vichy."

She told her mother about the prince in order to avoid talking to me. Her face glowed, and to hide her feeling she bent low over the table as though she were short-sighted, and made a show of reading the newspaper. My presence was disagreeable to her. I said good-bye and went home.

IV

It was quite still out of doors; the village on the further side of the pond was already asleep; there was not a light to be seen, and only the stars were faintly reflected in the pond. At the gate with the lions on it Genya was standing motionless, waiting to escort me.

"Every one is asleep in the village," I said to her,

trying to make out her face in the darkness, and I saw her mournful dark eyes fixed upon me. " The publican and the horse-stealers are asleep, while we, well-bred people, argue and irritate each other."

It was a melancholy August night — melancholy because there was already a feeling of autumn; the moon was rising behind a purple cloud, and it shed a faint light upon the road and on the dark fields of winter corn by the sides. From time to time a star fell. Genya walked beside me along the road, and tried not to look at the sky, that she might not see the falling stars, which for some reason frightened her.

" I believe you are right," she said, shivering with the damp night air. " If people, all together, could devote themselves to spiritual ends, they would soon know everything."

" Of course. We are higher beings, and if we were really to recognise the whole force of human genius and lived only for higher ends, we should in the end become like gods. But that will never be — mankind will degenerate till no traces of genius remain."

When the gates were out of sight, Genya stopped and shook hands with me.

" Good-night," she said, shivering; she had nothing but her blouse over her shoulders and was shrinking with cold. " Come to-morrow."

I felt wretched at the thought of being left alone, irritated and dissatisfied with myself and other peo-

ple; and I, too, tried not to look at the falling stars.
"Stay another minute," I said to her, "I entreat you."

I loved Genya. I must have loved her because she met me when I came and saw me off when I went away; because she looked at me tenderly and enthusiastically. How touchingly beautiful were her pale face, slender neck, slender arms, her weakness, her idleness, her reading. And intelligence? I suspected in her intelligence above the average. I was fascinated by the breadth of her views, perhaps because they were different from those of the stern, handsome Lida, who disliked me. Genya liked me, because I was an artist. I had conquered her heart by my talent, and had a passionate desire to paint for her sake alone; and I dreamed of her as of my little queen who with me would possess those trees, those fields, the mists, the dawn, the exquisite and beautiful scenery in the midst of which I had felt myself hopelessly solitary and useless.

"Stay another minute," I begged her. "I beseech you."

I took off my overcoat and put it over her chilly shoulders; afraid of looking ugly and absurd in a man's overcoat, she laughed, threw it off, and at that instant I put my arms round her and covered her face, shoulders, and hands with kisses.

"Till to-morrow," she whispered, and softly, as though afraid of breaking upon the silence of the night, she embraced me. "We have no secrets from one another. I must tell my mother and my sister at once. . . . It's so dreadful! Mother is all right; mother likes you — but Lida!"

She ran to the gates.

"Good-bye!" she called.

And then for two minutes I heard her running. I did not want to go home, and I had nothing to go for. I stood still for a little time hesitating, and made my way slowly back, to look once more at the house in which she lived, the sweet, simple old house, which seemed to be watching me from the windows of its upper storey, and understanding all about it. I walked by the terrace, sat on the seat by the tennis ground, in the dark under the old elm-tree, and looked from there at the house. In the windows of the top storey where Misuce slept there appeared a bright light, which changed to a soft green — they had covered the lamp with the shade. Shadows began to move. . . . I was full of tenderness, peace, and satisfaction with myself — satisfaction at having been able to be carried away by my feelings and having fallen in love, and at the same time I felt uncomfortable at the thought that only a few steps away from me, in one of the rooms of that house there was Lida, who disliked and perhaps hated me. I went on sitting there wondering whether Genya would come out; I listened and fancied I heard voices talking upstairs.

About an hour passed. The green light went out, and the shadows were no longer visible. The

moon was standing high above the house, and lighting up the sleeping garden and the paths; the dah-
lias and the roses in front of the house could be seen
distinctly, and looked all the same colour. It began to grow very cold. I went out of the garden,
picked up my coat on the road, and slowly sauntered
home.

When next day after dinner I went to the Voltchaninovs, the glass door into the garden was wide
open. I sat down on the terrace, expecting Genya
every minute, to appear from behind the flower-beds
on the lawn, or from one of the avenues, or that I
should hear her voice from the house. Then I
walked into the drawing-room, the dining-room.
There was not a soul to be seen. From the dining-
room I walked along the long corridor to the hall
and back. In this corridor there were several doors,
and through one of them I heard the voice of Lida:

" ' God . . . sent . . . a crow,' " she said in a
loud, emphatic voice, probably dictating — " ' God
sent a crow a piece of cheese. . . . A crow . . .
a piece of cheese.' . . . Who's there?" she called
suddenly, hearing my steps.

" It's I."

" Ah! Excuse me, I cannot come out to you this
minute; I'm giving Dasha her lesson."

" Is Ekaterina Pavlovna in the garden?"

" No, she went away with my sister this morning to our aunt in the province of Penza. And
in the winter they will probably go abroad," she

added after a pause. " ' God sent . . . the crow
. . . a piece . . . of cheese.' . . . Have you written it ? "

I went into the hall, and stared vacantly at the
pond and the village, and the sound reached me of
" A piece of cheese. . . . God sent the crow a
piece of cheese."

And I went back by the way I had come here for
the first time — first from the yard into the garden
past the house, then into the avenue of lime-trees.
. . . At this point I was overtaken by a small boy
who gave me a note:

" I told my sister everything and she insists on
my parting from you," I read. " I could not wound
her by disobeying. God will give you happiness.
Forgive me. If only you knew how bitterly my
mother and I are crying ! "

Then there was the dark fir avenue, the broken-
down fence. . . . On the field where then the rye
was in flower and the corncrakes were calling, now
there were cows and hobbled horses. On the slope
there were bright green patches of winter corn. A
sober workaday feeling came over me and I felt
ashamed of all I had said at the Voltchaninovs', and
felt bored with life as I had been before. When I
got home, I packed and set off that evening for Petersburg.

.   .   .   .

I never saw the Voltchaninovs again. Not long
ago, on my way to the Crimea, I met Byelokurov

in the train. As before, he was wearing a jerkin and an embroidered shirt, and when I asked how he was, he replied that, God be praised, he was well. We began talking. He had sold his old estate and bought another smaller one, in the name of Liubov Ivanovna. He could tell me little about the Voltchaninovs. Lida, he said, was still living in Shelkovka and teaching in the school; she had by degrees succeeded in gathering round her a circle of people sympathetic to her who made a strong party, and at the last election had turned out Balagin, who had till then had the whole district under his thumb. About Genya he only told me that she did not live at home, and that he did not know where she was.

I am beginning to forget the old house, and only sometimes when I am painting or reading I suddenly, apropos of nothing, remember the green light in the window, the sound of my footsteps as I walked home through the fields in the night, with my heart full of love, rubbing my hands in the cold. And still more rarely, at moments when I am sad and depressed by loneliness, I have dim memories, and little by little I begin to feel that she is thinking of me, too — that she is waiting for me, and that we shall meet. . . .

Misuce, where are you?

1896

THREE YEARS

THREE YEARS

I

IT was dark, and already lights had begun to gleam here and there in the houses, and a pale moon was rising behind the barracks at the end of the street. Laptev was sitting on a bench by the gate waiting for the end of the evening service at the Church of St. Peter and St. Paul. He was reckoning that Yulia Sergeyevna would pass by on her way from the service, and then he would speak to her, and perhaps spend the whole evening with her.

He had been sitting there for an hour and a half already, and all that time his imagination had been busy picturing his Moscow rooms, his Moscow friends, his man Pyotr, and his writing-table. He gazed half wonderingly at the dark, motionless trees, and it seemed strange to him that he was living now, not in his summer villa at Sokolniki, but in a provincial town in a house by which a great herd of cattle was driven every morning and evening, accompanied by terrible clouds of dust and the blowing of a horn. He thought of long conversations in which he had taken part quite lately in Moscow — conversations in which it had been maintained that one could live without love, that passionate love was an obsession, that finally there is no such love, but only a physical attraction between the sexes — and so on, in the same style; he remembered them and thought mournfully that if he were asked now what love was, he could not have found an answer.

The service was over, the people began to appear. Laptev strained his eyes gazing at the dark figures. The bishop had been driven by in his carriage, the bells had stopped ringing, and the red and green lights in the belfry were one after another extinguished — there had been an illumination, as it was dedication day — but the people were still coming out, lingering, talking, and standing under the windows.   But at last Laptev heard a familiar voice, his heart began beating violently, and he was overcome with despair on seeing that Yulia Sergeyevna was not alone, but walking with two ladies.

" It's awful, awful! " he whispered, feeling jealous.   " It's awful! "

At the corner of the lane, she stopped to say good-bye to the ladies, and while doing so glanced at Laptev.

" I was coming to see you," he said.   " I'm coming for a chat with your father.   Is he at home? "

" Most likely," she answered.   " It's early for him to have gone to the club."

There were gardens all along the lane, and a row of lime-trees growing by the fence cast a broad patch of shadow in the moonlight, so that the gate and the fences were completely plunged in darkness on one side, from which came the sounds of women whispering, smothered laughter, and someone playing softly on a balalaika. There was a fragrance of lime-flowers and of hay. This fragrance and the murmur of the unseen whispers worked upon Laptev. He was all at once overwhelmed with a passionate longing to throw his arms round his companion, to shower kisses on her face, her hands, her shoulders, to burst into sobs, to fall at her feet and to tell her how long he had been waiting for her. A faint scarcely perceptible scent of incense hung about her; and that scent reminded him of the time when he, too, believed in God and used to go to evening service, and when he used to dream so much of pure romantic love. And it seemed to him that, because this girl did not love him, all possibility of the happiness he had dreamed of then was lost to him forever.

She began speaking sympathetically of the illness of his sister, Nina Fyodorovna. Two months before his sister had undergone an operation for cancer, and now every one was expecting a return of the disease.

"I went to see her this morning," said Yulia Sergeyevna, "and it seemed to me that during the last week she has, not exactly grown thin, but has, as it were, faded."

"Yes, yes," Laptev agreed. "There's no return of the symptoms, but every day I notice she grows weaker and weaker, and is wasting before my eyes. I don't understand what's the matter with her."

" Oh dear! And how strong she used to be, plump and rosy!" said Yulia Sergeyevna after a moment's silence. " Every one here used to call her the Moscow lady. How she used to laugh! On holidays she used to dress up like a peasant girl, and it suited her so well."

Doctor Sergey Borisovitch was at home; he was a stout, red-faced man, wearing a long coat that reached below his knees, and looking as though he had short legs. He was pacing up and down his study, with his hands in his pockets, and humming to himself in an undertone, " Ru-ru-ru-ru." His grey whiskers looked unkempt, and his hair was unbrushed, as though he had just got out of bed. And his study with pillows on the sofa, with stacks of papers in the corners, and with a dirty invalid poodle lying under the table, produced the same impression of unkemptness and untidiness as himself.

" M. Laptev wants to see you," his daughter said to him, going into his study.

" Ru-ru-ru-ru," he hummed louder than ever, and turning into the drawing-room, gave his hand to Laptev, and asked: " What good news have you to tell me? "

It was dark in the drawing-room. Laptev, still standing with his hat in his hand, began apologising for disturbing him; he asked what was to be done to make his sister sleep at night, and why she was growing so thin; and he was embarrassed by the thought that he had asked those very questions at his visit that morning.

" Tell me," he said, " wouldn't it be as well to send for some specialist on internal diseases from Moscow? What do you think of it? "

The doctor sighed, shrugged his shoulders, and made a vague gesture with his hands.

It was evident that he was offended. He was a very huffy man, prone to take offence, and always ready to suspect that people did not believe in him, that he was not recognised or properly respected, that his patients exploited him, and that his colleagues showed him ill-will. He was always jeering at himself, saying that fools like him were only made for the public to ride rough-shod over them.

Yulia Sergeyevna lighted the lamp. She was tired out with the service, and that was evident from her pale, exhausted face, and her weary step. She wanted to rest. She sat down on the sofa, put her hands on her lap, and sank into thought. Laptev knew that he was ugly, and now he felt as though he were conscious of his ugliness all over his body. He was short, thin, with ruddy cheeks, and his hair had grown so thin that his head felt cold. In his expression there was none of that refined simplicity which makes even rough, ugly faces attractive; in the society of women, he was awkward, over-talkative, affected. And now he almost despised himself for it. He must talk that Yulia Sergeyevna might not be bored in his company. But what about? About his sister's illness again?

And he began to talk about medicine, saying what is usually said. He approved of hygiene, and said that he had long ago wanted to found a night-refuge in Moscow — in fact, he had already calculated the cost of it. According to his plan the workmen who came in the evening to the night-refuge were to receive a supper of hot cabbage soup with bread, a warm, dry bed with a rug, and a place for drying their clothes and their boots.

Yulia Sergeyevna was usually silent in his presence, and in a strange way, perhaps by the instinct of a lover, he divined her thoughts and intentions. And now, from the fact that after the evening service she had not gone to her room to change her dress and drink tea, he deduced that she was going to pay some visit elsewhere.

" But I'm in no hurry with the night-refuge," he went on, speaking with vexation and irritability, and addressing the doctor, who looked at him, as it were, blankly and in perplexity, evidently unable to understand what induced him to raise the question of medicine and hygiene. " And most likely it will be a long time, too, before I make use of our estimate. I fear our night-shelter will fall into the hands of our pious humbugs and philanthropic ladies, who always ruin any undertaking."

Yulia Sergeyevna got up and held out her hand to Laptev.

"Excuse me," she said, "it's time for me to go. Please give my love to your sister."

"Ru-ru-ru-ru," hummed the doctor. "Ru-ru-ru-ru."

Yulia Sergeyevna went out, and after staying a little longer, Laptev said good-bye to the doctor and went home. When a man is dissatisfied and feels unhappy, how trivial seem to him the shapes of the lime-trees, the shadows, the clouds, all the beauties of nature, so complacent, so indifferent! By now the moon was high up in the sky, and the clouds were scudding quickly below. "But how naïve and provincial the moon is, how threadbare and paltry the clouds!" thought Laptev. He felt ashamed of the way he had talked just now about medicine, and the night-refuge. He felt with horror that next day he would not have will enough to resist trying to see her and talk to her again, and would again be convinced that he was nothing to her. And the day after — it would be the same. With what object? And how and when would it all end?

At home he went in to see his sister. Nina Fyodorovna still looked strong and gave the impression of being a well-built, vigorous woman, but her striking pallor made her look like a corpse, especially when, as now, she was lying on her back with her eyes closed; her eldest daughter Sasha, a girl of ten years old, was sitting beside her reading aloud from her reading-book.

" Alyosha has come," the invalid said softly to herself.

There had long been established between Sasha and her uncle a tacit compact, to take turns in sitting with the patient.   On this occasion Sasha closed her reading-book, and without uttering a word, went softly out of the room.   Laptev took an historical novel from the chest of drawers, and looking for the right page, sat down and began reading it aloud.

Nina Fyodorovna was born in Moscow of a merchant family.   She and her two brothers had spent their childhood and early youth, living at home in Pyatnitsky Street.   Their childhood was long and wearisome; her father treated her sternly, and had even on two or three occasions flogged her, and her mother had had a long illness and died.   The servants were coarse, dirty, and hypocritical; the house was frequented by priests and monks, also hypocritical; they ate and drank and coarsely flattered her father, whom they did not like.   The boys had the good-fortune to go to school, while Nina was left practically uneducated.   All her life she wrote an illegible scrawl, and had read nothing but historical novels.   Seventeen years ago, when she was twenty-two, on a summer holiday at Himki, she made the acquaintance of her present husband, a landowner called Panaurov, had fallen in love with him, and married him secretly against her father's will. Panaurov, a handsome, rather impudent fellow, who whistled and lighted his cigarette from the holy lamp, struck the father as an absolutely worthless person. And when the son-in-law began in his letters demanding a dowry, the old man wrote to his daughter that he would send her furs, silver, and various articles that had been left at her mother's death, as well as thirty thousand roubles, but without his paternal blessing. Later he sent another twenty thousand. This money, as well as the dowry, was spent; the estate had been sold and Panaurov moved with his family to the town and got a job in a provincial government office. In the town he formed another tie, and had a second family, and this was the subject of much talk, as his illicit family was not a secret.

Nina Fyodorovna adored her husband. And now, listening to the historical novel, she was thinking how much she had gone through in her life, how much she had suffered, and that if any one were to describe her life it would make a very pathetic story. As the tumour was in her breast, she was persuaded that love and her domestic grief were the cause of her illness, and that jealousy and tears had brought her to her hopeless state.

At last Alexey Fyodorovitch closed the book and said:

" That's the end, and thank God for it. To-morrow we'll begin a new one."

Nina Fyodorovna laughed. She had always been given to laughter, but of late Laptev had begun to notice that at moments her mind seemed weakened by illness, and she would laugh at the smallest trifle, and even without any cause at all.

"Yulia came before dinner while you were out," she said. "So far as I can see, she hasn't much faith in her papa. 'Let papa go on treating you,' she said, 'but write in secret to the holy elder to pray for you, too.' There is a holy man somewhere here. Yulia forgot her parasol here; you must take it to her to-morrow," she went on after a brief pause. "No, when the end comes, neither doctors nor holy men are any help."

"Nina, why can't you sleep at night?" Laptev asked, to change the subject.

"Oh, well, I don't go to sleep — that's all. I lie and think."

"What do you think about, dear?"

"About the children, about you . . . about my life. I've gone through a great deal, Alyosha, you know. When one begins to remember and remember. . . . My God!" She laughed. "It's no joke to have borne five children as I have, to have buried three. . . . Sometimes I was expecting to be confined while my Grigory Nikolaitch would be sitting at that very time with another woman. There would be no one to send for the doctor or the midwife. I would go into the passage or the kitchen for the servant, and there Jews, tradesmen, moneylenders, would be waiting for him to come home. My head used to go round. . . . He did not love me, though he never said so openly. Now I've grown calmer — it doesn't weigh on my heart; but in old days, when I was younger, it hurt me — ach! how it hurt me, darling! Once — while we were still in the country — I found him in the garden with a lady, and I walked away. . . . I walked on aimlessly, and I don't know how, but I found myself in the church porch. I fell on my knees: ' Queen of Heaven! ' I said. And it was night, the moon was shining. . . ."

She was exhausted, she began gasping for breath. Then, after resting a little, she took her brother's hand and went on in a weak, toneless voice:

"How kind you are, Aloysha! . . . And how clever! . . . What a good man you've grown up into! "

At midnight Laptev said good-night to her, and as he went away he took with him the parasol that Yulia Sergeyevna had forgotten. In spite of the late hour, the servants, male and female, were drinking tea in the dining-room. How disorderly! The children were not in bed, but were there in the dining-room, too. They were all talking softly in undertones, and had not noticed that the lamp was smoking and would soon go out. All these people, big and little, were disturbed by a whole succession of bad omens and were in an oppressed mood. The glass in the hall had been broken, the samovar had been buzzing every day, and, as though on purpose, was even buzzing now. They were describing how a mouse had jumped out of Nina Fyodorovna's boot when she was dressing. And the children were quite aware of the terrible significance of these omens. The elder girl, Sasha, a thin little brunette, was sitting motionless at the table, and her face looked scared and woebegone, while the younger, Lida, a chubby fair child of seven, stood beside her sister looking from under her brows at the light.

Laptev went downstairs to his own rooms in the lower storey, where under the low ceilings it was always close and smelt of geraniums. In his sitting-room, Panaurov, Nina Fyodorovna's husband, was sitting reading the newspaper. Laptev nodded to him and sat down opposite. Both sat still and said nothing. They used to spend whole evenings like this without speaking, and neither of them was in the least put out by this silence.

The little girls came down from upstairs to say good-night. Deliberately and in silence, Panaurov made the sign of the cross over them several times, and gave them his hand to kiss. They dropped curtsies, and then went up to Laptev, who had to make the sign of the cross and give them his hand to kiss also. This ceremony with the hand-kissing and curtsying was repeated every evening.

When the children had gone out Panaurov laid aside the newspaper and said:

"It's not very lively in our God-fearing town! I must confess, my dear fellow," he added with a sigh, "I'm very glad that at last you've found some distraction."

"What do you mean?" asked Laptev.

"I saw you coming out of Dr. Byelavin's just now. I expect you don't go there for the sake of the papa."

"Of course not," said Laptev, and he blushed.

"Well, of course not. And by the way, you wouldn't find such another old brute as that papa if you hunted by daylight with a candle. You can't imagine what a foul, stupid, clumsy beast he is! You cultured people in the capitals are still interested in the provinces only on the lyrical side, only from the *paysage* and *Poor Anton* point of view, but I can assure you, my boy, there's nothing logical about it; there's nothing but barbarism, meanness, and nastiness — that's all. Take the local devotees of science — the local intellectuals, so to speak. Can you imagine there are here in this town twenty-eight doctors? They've all made their fortunes, and they are living in houses of their own, and meanwhile the population is in just as helpless a condition as ever. Here, Nina had to have an operation, quite an ordinary one really, yet we were obliged to get a surgeon from Moscow; not one doctor here would undertake it. It's beyond all conception. They know nothing, they understand nothing. They take no interest in anything. Ask them, for instance, what cancer is — what it is, what it comes from."

And Panaurov began to explain what cancer was. He was a specialist on all scientific subjects, and explained from a scientific point of view everything that was discussed.   But he explained it all in his own way.   He had a theory of his own about the circulation of the blood, about chemistry, about astronomy.   He talked slowly, softly, convincingly.

" It's beyond all conception," he pronounced in an imploring voice, screwing up his eyes, sighing languidly, and smiling as graciously as a king, and it was evident that he was very well satisfied with himself, and never gave a thought to the fact that he was fifty.

" I am rather hungry," said Laptev.   " I should like something savoury."

" Well, that can easily be managed."

Not long afterwards Laptev and his brother-in-law were sitting upstairs in the dining-room having supper.   Laptev had a glass of vodka, and then began drinking wine.   Panaurov drank nothing. He never drank, and never gambled, yet in spite of that he had squandered all his own and his wife's property, and had accumulated debts.   To squander so much in such a short time, one must have, not passions, but a special talent.   Panaurov liked dainty fare, liked a handsome dinner service, liked music after dinner, speeches, bowing footmen, to whom he would carelessly fling tips of ten, even twenty-five roubles. He always took part in all lotteries and subscriptions, sent bouquets to ladies of his acquaintance on their birthdays, bought cups, stands for glasses, studs, ties, walking-sticks, scents, cigarette-holders, pipes, lap-dogs, parrots, Japanese bric-à-brac, antiques; he had silk nightshirts, and a bedstead made of ebony inlaid with mother-of-pearl. His dressing-gown was a genuine Bokhara, and everything was to correspond; and on all this there went every day, as he himself expressed, " a deluge " of money.

At supper he kept sighing and shaking his head.

" Yes, everything on this earth has an end," he said softly, screwing up his dark eyes. " You will fall in love and suffer. You will fall out of love; you'll be deceived, for there is no woman who will not deceive; you will suffer, will be brought to despair, and will be faithless too. But the time will come when all this will be a memory, and when you will reason about it coldly and look upon it as utterly trivial. . . ."

Laptev, tired, a little drunk, looked at his handsome head, his clipped black beard, and seemed to understand why women so loved this pampered, conceited, and physically handsome creature.

After supper Panaurov did not stay in the house, but went off to his other lodgings. Laptev went out to see him on his way. Panaurov was the only man in the town who wore a top-hat, and his elegant, dandified figure, his top-hat and tan gloves, beside the grey fences, the pitiful little houses, with their three windows and the thickets of nettles, always made a strange and mournful impression.

After saying good-bye to him Laptev returned home without hurrying. The moon was shining brightly; one could distinguish every straw on the ground, and Laptev felt as though the moonlight were caressing his bare head, as though some one were passing a feather over his hair.

" I love ! " he pronounced aloud, and he had a sudden longing to run to overtake Panaurov, to embrace him, to forgive him, to make him a present of a lot of money, and then to run off into the open country, into a wood, to run on and on without looking back.

At home he saw lying on the chair the parasol Yulia Sergeyevna had forgotten; he snatched it up and kissed it greedily. The parasol was a silk one, no longer new, tied round with old elastic. The handle was a cheap one, of white bone. Laptev opened it over him, and he felt as though there were the fragrance of happiness about him.

He settled himself more comfortably in his chair, and still keeping hold of the parasol, began writing to Moscow to one of his friends:

" DEAR PRECIOUS KOSTYA,

" Here is news for you: I'm in love again!   I say *again*, because six years ago I fell in love with a

Moscow actress, though I didn't even succeed in
making her acquaintance, and for· the last year and
a half I have been living with a certain person you
know — a woman neither young nor good-looking.
Ah, my dear boy, how unlucky I am in love. I've
never had any success with women, and if I say
again it's simply because it's rather sad and mortify-
ing to acknowledge even to myself that my youth
has passed entirely without love, and that I'm in
love in a real sense now for the first time in my life,
at thirty-four. Let it stand that I love *again*.

"If only you knew what a girl she was! She
couldn't be called a beauty — she has a broad face,
she is very thin, but what a wonderful expression
of goodness she has when she smiles! When she
speaks; her voice is as clear as a bell. She never
carries on a conversation with me — I don't know
her; but when I'm beside her I feel she's a striking,
exceptional creature, full of intelligence and lofty
aspirations. She is religious, and you cannot
imagine how deeply this touches me and exalts her
in my eyes. On that point I am ready to argue with
you endlessly. You may be right, to your thinking; but, still, I love to see her praying in church.
She is a provincial, but she was educated in Moscow.
She loves our Moscow; she dresses in the Moscow
style, and I love her for that — love her, love her.
. . . I see you frowning and getting up to read
me a long lecture on what love is, and what sort of

woman one can love, and what sort one cannot, and
so on, and so on.   But, dear Kostya, before I was
in love I, too, knew quite well what love was.

" My sister thanks you for your message.   She
often recalls how she used to take Kostya Kotchevoy to the preparatory class, and never speaks of
you except as *poor Kostya*, as she still thinks of you
as the little orphan boy she remembers.   And so,
poor orphan, I'm in love.   While it's a secret, don't
say anything to a ' certain person.'   I think it will
all come right of itself, or, as the footman says in
Tolstoy, will ' come round.' "

When he had finished his letter Laptev went to
bed.   He was so tired that he couldn't keep his
eyes open, but for some reason he could not get to
sleep; the noise in the street seemed to prevent him.
The cattle were driven by to the blowing of a horn,
and soon afterwards the bells began ringing for
early mass.   At one minute a cart drove by creak-
ing; at the next, he heard the voice of some woman
going to market.   And the sparrows twittered the
whole time.

II

The next morning was a cheerful one; it was a
holiday.   At ten o'clock Nina Fyodorovna, wearing a brown dress and with her hair neatly arranged,
was led into the drawing-room, supported on each

side. There she walked about a little and stood
by the open window, and her smile was broad and
naïve, and, looking at her, one recalled a local artist, a great drunkard, who wanted her to sit to
him for a picture of the Russian carnival.   And all
of them — the children, the servants, her brother,
Alexey Fyodorovitch, and she herself — were suddenly convinced, that she was certainly going to get
well. With shrieks of laughter the children ran
after their uncle, chasing him and catching him, and
filling the house with noise.

People called to ask how she was, brought her
holy bread, told her that in almost all the churches
they were offering up prayers for her that day.
She had been conspicuous for her benevolence in
the town, and was liked.   She was very ready with
her charity, like her brother Alexey, who gave away
his money freely, without considering whether it
was necessary to give it or not.   Nina Fyodorovna
used to pay the school fees for poor children; used
to give away tea, sugar, and jam to old women;
used to provide trousseaux for poor brides; and if
she picked up a newspaper, she always looked first
of all to see if there were any appeals for charity
or a paragraph about somebody's being in a desti-
tute condition.

She was holding now in her hand a bundle of
notes, by means of which various poor people, her
protégés, had procured goods from a grocer's shop.

They had been sent her the evening before by the shopkeeper with a request for the payment of the total — eighty-two roubles.

"My goodness, what a lot they've had! They've no conscience!" she said, deciphering with difficulty her ugly handwriting. "It's no joke! Eighty-two roubles! I declare I won't pay it."

"I'll pay it to-day," said Laptev.

"Why should you? Why should you?" cried Nina Fyodorovna in agitation. "It's quite enough for me to take two hundred and fifty every month from you and our brother. God bless you!" she added, speaking softly, so as not to be overheard by the servants.

"Well, but I spend two thousand five hundred a month," he said. "I tell you again, dear: you have just as much right to spend it as I or Fyodor. Do understand that, once for all. There are three of us, and of every three kopecks of our father's money, one belongs to you."

But Nina Fyodorovna did not understand, and her expression looked as though she were mentally solving some very difficult problem. And this lack of comprehension in pecuniary matters, always made Laptev feel uneasy and troubled. He suspected that she had private debts in addition which worried her and of which she scrupled to tell him.

Then came the sound of footsteps and heavy breathing; it was the doctor coming up the stairs, dishevelled and unkempt as usual.

" Ru-ru-ru," he was humming. " Ru-ru."

To avoid meeting him, Laptev went into the dining-room, and then went downstairs to his own room. It was clear to him that to get on with the doctor and to drop in at his house without formalities was impossible; and to meet the " old brute," as Panaurov called him, was distasteful. That was why he so rarely saw Yulia. He reflected now that the father was not at home, that if he were to take Yulia Sergeyevna her parasol, he would be sure to find her at home alone, and his heart ached with joy. Haste, haste!

He took the parasol and, violently agitated, flew on the wings of love. It was hot in the street. In the big courtyard of the doctor's house, overgrown with coarse grass and nettles, some twenty urchins were playing ball. These were all the children of working-class families who tenanted the three disreputable-looking lodges, which the doctor was always meaning to have done up, though he put it off from year to year. The yard resounded with ringing, healthy voices. At some distance on one side, Yulia Sergeyevna was standing at her porch, her hands folded, watching the game.

" Good-morning! " Laptev called to her.

She looked round. Usually he saw her indifferent, cold, or tired as she had been the evening before. Now her face looked full of life and frolic, like the faces of the boys who were playing ball.

" Look, they never play so merrily in Moscow,"

she said, going to meet him. "There are no such big yards there, though; they've no place to run there. Papa has only just gone to you," she added, looking round at the children.

"I know; but I've not come to see him, but to see you," said Laptev, admiring her youthfulness, which he had not noticed till then, and seemed only that day to have discovered in her; it seemed to him as though he were seeing her slender white neck with the gold chain for the first time. "I've come to see you . . ." he repeated. "My sister has sent you your parasol; you forgot it yesterday."

She put out her hand to take the parasol, but he pressed it to his bosom and spoke passionately, without restraint, yielding again to the sweet ecstasy he had felt the night before, sitting under the parasol.

"I entreat you, give it me. I shall keep it in memory of you . . . of our acquaintance. It's so wonderful!"

"Take it," she said, and blushed; "but there's nothing wonderful about it."

He looked at her in ecstasy, in silence, not knowing what to say.

"Why am I keeping you here in the heat?" she said after a brief pause, laughing. "Let us go indoors."

"I am not disturbing you?"

They went into the hall. Yulia Sergeyevna ran

upstairs, her white dress with blue flowers on it rustling as she went.

" I can't be disturbed," she answered, stopping on the landing. " I never do anything. Every day is a holiday for me, from morning till night."

" What you say is inconceivable to me," he said, going up to her. " I grew up in a world in which every one without exception, men and women alike, worked hard every day."

" But if one has nothing to do? " she asked.

" One has to arrange one's life under such conditions, that work is inevitable. There can be no clean and happy life without work."

Again he pressed the parasol to his bosom, and to his own surprise spoke softly, in a voice unlike his own:

" If you would consent to be my wife I would give everything — I would give everything. There's no price I would not pay, no sacrifice I would not make."

She started and looked at him with wonder and alarm.

" What are you saying! " she brought out, turning pale. " It's impossible, I assure you. Forgive me."

Then with the same rustle of her skirts she went up higher, and vanished through the doorway.

Laptev grasped what this meant, and his mood was transformed, completely, abruptly, as though a light in his soul had suddenly been extinguished.

Filled with the shame of a man humiliated, of a man who is disdained, who is not liked, who is distasteful, perhaps disgusting, who is shunned, he walked out of the house.

" I would give everything," he thought, mimicking himself as he went home through the heat and recalled the details of his declaration. " I would give everything — like a regular tradesman. As though she wanted your *everything!* "

All he had just said seemed to him repulsively stupid. Why had he lied, saying that he had grown up in a world where every one worked, without exception? Why had he talked to her in a lecturing tone about a clean and happy life? It was not clever, not interesting; it was false — false in the Moscow style. But by degrees there followed that mood of indifference into which criminals sink after a severe sentence. He began thinking that, thank God! everything was at an end and that the terrible uncertainty was over; that now there was no need to spend whole days in anticipation, in pining, in thinking always of the same thing. Now everything was clear; he must give up all hope of personal happiness, live without desires, without hopes, without dreams, or expectations, and to escape that dreary sadness which he was so sick of trying to soothe, he could busy himself with other people's affairs, other people's happiness, and old age would come on imperceptibly, and life would reach its end —

and nothing more was wanted. He did not care, he wished for nothing, and could reason about it coolly, but there was a sort of heaviness in his face especially under his eyes, his forehead felt drawn tight like elastic — and tears were almost starting into his eyes. Feeling weak all over, he lay down on his bed, and in five minutes was sound asleep.

III

The proposal Laptev had made so suddenly threw Yulia Sergeyevna into despair.

She knew Laptev very little, had made his acquaintance by chance; he was a rich man, a partner in the well-known Moscow firm of "Fyodor Laptev and Sons"; always serious, apparently clever, and anxious about his sister's illness. It had seemed to her that he took no notice of her whatever, and she did not care about him in the least — and then all of a sudden that declaration on the stairs, that pitiful, ecstatic face. . . .

The offer had overwhelmed her by its suddenness and by the fact that the word *wife* had been uttered, and by the necessity of rejecting it. She could not remember what she had said to Laptev, but she still felt traces of the sudden, unpleasant feeling with which she had rejected him. He did not attract her; he looked like a shopman; he was not interesting; she could not have answered him except with a refusal, and yet she felt uncomfortable, as though she had done wrong.

"My God! without waiting to get into the room, on the stairs," she said to herself in despair, addressing the ikon which hung over her pillow; "and no courting beforehand, but so strangely, so oddly. . . ."

In her solitude her agitation grew more intense every hour, and it was beyond her strength to master this oppressive feeling alone. She needed some one to listen to her story and to tell her that she had done right. But she had no one to talk to. She had lost her mother long before; she thought her father a queer man, and could not talk to him seriously. He worried her with his whims, his extreme readiness to take offence, and his meaningless gestures; and as soon as one began to talk to him, he promptly turned the conversation on himself. And in her prayer she was not perfectly open, because she did not know for certain what she ought to pray for.

The samovar was brought in. Yulia Sergeyevna, very pale and tired, looking dejected, came into the dining-room to make tea — it was one of her duties — and poured out a glass for her father. Sergey Borisovitch, in his long coat that reached below his knees, with his red face and unkempt hair, walked up and down the room with his hands in his pockets, pacing, not from corner to corner, but backwards and forwards at random, like a wild beast in its cage. He would stand still by the table, sip his glass of tea with relish, and pace about again, lost in thought.

"Laptev made me an offer to-day," said Yulia Sergeyevna, and she flushed crimson.

The doctor looked at her and did not seem to understand.

"Laptev?" he queried. "Panaurov's brother-in-law?"

He was fond of his daughter; it was most likely that she would sooner or later be married, and leave him, but he tried not to think about that. He was afraid of being alone, and for some reason fancied, that if he were left alone in that great house, he would have an apoplectic stroke, but he did not like to speak of this directly.

"Well, I'm delighted to hear it," he said, shrugging his shoulders. "I congratulate you with all my heart. It offers you a splendid opportunity for leaving me, to your great satisfaction. And I quite understand your feelings. To live with an old father, an invalid, half crazy, must be very irksome at your age. I quite understand you. And the sooner I'm laid out and in the devil's clutches, the better every one will be pleased. I congratulate you with all my heart."

"I refused him."

The doctor felt relieved, but he was unable to stop himself and went on:

"I wonder, I've long wondered, why I've not yet

been put into a madhouse — why I'm still wearing
this coat instead of a strait-waistcoat?   I still have
faith in justice, in goodness.   I am a fool, an ideal-
ist, and nowadays that's insanity, isn't it?   And how
do they repay me for my honesty?   They almost
throw stones at me and ride rough-shod over me.
And even my nearest kith and kin do nothing but
try to get the better of me.   It's high time the devil
fetched an old fool like me. . . ."

"There's no talking to you like a rational being!" said Yulia.

She got up from the table impulsively, and went
to her room in great wrath, remembering how often
her father had been unjust to her.   But a little while
afterwards she felt sorry for her father, too, and
when he was going to the club she went downstairs
with him, and shut the door after him.   It was a
rough and stormy night; the door shook with the
violence of the wind, and there were draughts in all
directions in the passage, so that the candle was almost blown out.   In her own domain upstairs Yulia
Sergeyevna went the round of all the rooms, making
the sign of the cross over every door and window;
the wind howled, and it sounded as though some one
were walking on the roof.   Never had it been so
dreary, never had she felt so lonely.

She asked herself whether she had done right
in rejecting a man, simply because his appearance
did not attract her.   It was true he was a man
she did not love, and to marry him would mean re-

nouncing forever her dreams, her conceptions of happiness in married life, but would she ever meet the man of whom she dreamed, and would he love her? She was twenty-one already. There were no eligible young men in the town. She pictured all the men she knew — government clerks, schoolmasters, officers, and some of them were married already, and their domestic life was conspicuous for its dreariness and triviality; others were uninteresting, colourless, unintelligent, immoral. Laptev was, anyway, a Moscow man, had taken his degree at the university, spoke French. He lived in the capital, where there were lots of clever, noble, remarkable people; where there was noise and bustle, splendid theatres, musical evenings, first-rate dressmakers, confectioners. . . . In the Bible it was written that a wife must love her husband, and great importance was given to love in novels, but wasn't there exaggeration in it? Was it out of the question to enter upon married life without love? It was said, of course, that love soon passed away, and that nothing was left but habit, and that the object of married life was not to be found in love, nor in happiness, but in duties, such as the bringing up of one's children, the care of one's household, and so on. And perhaps what was meant in the Bible was love for one's husband as one's neighbour, respect for him, charity.

At night Yulia Sergeyevna read the evening prayers attentively, then knelt down, and pressing her hands to her bosom, gazing at the flame of the lamp before the ikon, said with feeling:

"Give me understanding, Holy Mother, our Defender! Give me understanding, O Lord!"

She had in the course of her life come across elderly maiden ladies, poor and of no consequence in the world, who bitterly repented and openly confessed their regret that they had refused suitors in the past. Would not the same thing happen to her? Had not she better go into a convent or become a Sister of Mercy?

She undressed and got into bed, crossing herself and crossing the air around her. Suddenly the bell rang sharply and plaintively in the corridor.

"Oh, my God!" she said, feeling a nervous irritation all over her at the sound. She lay still and kept thinking how poor this provincial life was in events, monotonous and yet not peaceful. One was constantly having to tremble, to feel apprehensive, angry or guilty, and in the end one's nerves were so strained, that one was afraid to peep out of the bedclothes.

A little while afterwards the bell rang just as sharply again. The servant must have been asleep and had not heard. Yulia Sergeyevna lighted a candle, and feeling vexed with the servant, began with a shiver to dress, and when she went out into the corridor, the maid was already closing the door downstairs.

" I thought it was the master, but it's some one from a patient," she said.

Yulia Sergeyevna went back to her room. She took a pack of cards out of the chest of drawers, and decided that if after shuffling the cards well and cutting, the bottom card turned out to be a red one, it would mean *yes* — that is, she would accept Laptev's offer; and that if it was a black, it would mean *no*. The card turned out to be the ten of spades.

That relieved her mind — she fell asleep; but in the morning, she was wavering again between *yes* and *no*, and she was dwelling on the thought that she could, if she chose, change her life. The thought harassed her, she felt exhausted and unwell; but yet, soon after eleven, she dressed and went to see Nina Fyodorovna. She wanted to see Laptev: perhaps now he would seem more attractive to her; perhaps she had been wrong about him hitherto. . . .

She found it hard to walk against the wind. She struggled along, holding her hat on with both hands, and could see nothing for the dust.

IV

Going into his sister's room, and seeing to his surprise Yulia Sergeyevna, Laptev had again the humiliating sensation of a man who feels himself an object of repulsion. He concluded that if after what had happened yesterday she could bring herself so easily to visit his sister and meet him, it must be because she was not concerned about him, and regarded him as a complete nonentity. But when he greeted her, and with a pale face and dust under her eyes she looked at him mournfully and remorsefully, he saw that she, too, was miserable.

She did not feel well. She only stayed ten minutes, and began saying good-bye. And as she went out she said to Laptev:

" Will you see me home, Alexey Fyodorovitch? "

They walked along the street in silence, holding their hats, and, he, walking a little behind, tried to screen her from the wind. In the lane it was more sheltered, and they walked side by side.

" Forgive me if I was not nice yesterday;" and her voice quavered as though she were going to cry. " I was so wretched! I did not sleep all night."

" I slept well all night," said Laptev, without looking at her; " but that doesn't mean that I was happy. My life is broken. I'm deeply unhappy, and after your refusal yesterday I go about like a man poisoned. The most difficult thing was said yesterday. To-day I feel no embarrassment and can talk to you frankly. I love you more than my sister, more than my dead mother. . . . I can live without my sister, and without my mother, and I have lived without them, but life without you — is meaningless to me; I can't face it. . . ."

And now too, as usual, he guessed her intention.

He realised that she wanted to go back to what had happened the day before, and with that object had asked him to accompany her, and now was taking him home with her. But what could she add to her refusal? What new idea had she in her head? From everything, from her glances, from her smile, and even from her tone, from the way she held her head and shoulders as she walked beside him, he saw that, as before, she did not love him, that he was a stranger to her. What more did she want to say?

Doctor Sergey Borisovitch was at home.

" You are very welcome. I'm always glad to see you, Fyodor Alexeyitch," he said, mixing up his Christian name and his father's. " Delighted, delighted!"

He had never been so polite before, and Laptev saw that he knew of his offer; he did not like that either. He was sitting now in the drawing-room, and the room impressed him strangely, with its poor, common decorations, its wretched pictures, and though there were arm-chairs in it, and a huge lamp with a shade over it, it still looked like an uninhabited place, a huge barn, and it was obvious that no one could feel at home in such a room, except a man like the doctor. The next room, almost twice as large, was called the reception-room, and in it there were only rows of chairs, as though for a dancing class. And while Laptev was sitting in the drawing-room talking to the doctor about his sis-

ter, he began to be tortured by a suspicion. Had
not Yulia Sergeyevna been to his sister Nina's, and
then brought him here to tell him that she would accept him?   Oh, how awful it was!   But the most
awful thing of all was that his soul was capable of
such a suspicion.   And he imagined how the father
and the daughter had spent the evening, and perhaps
the night before, in prolonged consultation, perhaps
dispute, and at last had come to the conclusion that
Yulia had acted thoughtlessly in refusing a rich man.
The words that parents use in such cases kept ringing in his ears:

" It is true you don't love him, but think what
good you could do ! "

The doctor was going out to see patients.   Laptev would have gone with him, but Yulia Sergeyevna
said:

" I beg you to stay."

She was distressed and dispirited, and told herself now that to refuse an honourable, good man who
loved her, simply because he was not attractive, especially when marrying him would make it possible
for her to change her mode of life, her cheerless,
monotonous, idle life in which youth was passing
with no prospect of anything better in the future —
to refuse him under such circumstances was madness, caprice and folly, and that God might even pun-
ish her for it.

The father went out.   When the sound of his
steps had died away, she suddenly stood up before

Laptev and said resolutely, turning horribly white as she did so:

"I thought for a long time yesterday, Alexey Fyodorovitch. . . . I accept your offer."

He bent down and kissed her hand. She kissed him awkwardly on the head with cold lips.

He felt that in this love scene the chief thing — her love — was lacking, and that there was a great deal that was not wanted; and he longed to cry out, to run away, to go back to Moscow at once. But she was close to him, and she seemed to him so lovely, and he was suddenly overcome by passion. He reflected that it was too late for deliberation now; he embraced her passionately, and muttered some words, calling her *thou;* he kissed her on the neck, and then on the cheek, on the head. . . .

She walked away to the window, dismayed by these demonstrations, and both of them were already regretting what they had said and both were asking themselves in confusion:

"Why has this happened?"

"If only you knew how miserable I am!" she said, wringing her hands.

"What is it?" he said, going up to her, wringing his hands too. "My dear, for God's sake, tell me — what is it? Only tell the truth, I entreat you — nothing but the truth!"

"Don't pay any attention to it," she said, and forced herself to smile. "I promise you I'll be a faithful, devoted wife. . . . Come this evening."

Sitting afterwards with his sister and reading aloud an historical novel, he recalled it all and felt wounded that his splendid, pure, rich feeling was met with such a shallow response. He was not loved, but his offer had been accepted — in all probability because he was rich: that is, what was thought most of in him was what he valued least of all in himself. It was quite possible that Yulia, who was so pure and believed in God, had not once thought of his money; but she did not love him — did not love him, and evidently she had interested motives, vague, perhaps, and not fully thought out — still, it was so. The doctor's house with its common furniture was repulsive to him, and he looked upon the doctor himself as a wretched, greasy miser, a sort of operatic Gaspard from " Les Cloches de Corneville." The very name " Yulia " had a vulgar sound. He imagined how he and his Yulia would stand at their wedding, in reality complete strangers to one another, without a trace of feeling on her side, just as though their marriage had been made by a professional matchmaker; and the only consolation left him now, as commonplace as the marriage itself, was the reflection that he was not the first, and would not be the last; that thousands of people were married like that; and that with time, when Yulia came to know him better, she would perhaps grow fond of him.

" Romeo and Juliet! " he said, as he shut the novel, and he laughed. " I am Romeo, Nina.

You may congratulate me.   I made an offer to Yulia
Byelavin to-day."

Nina Fyodorovna thought he was joking, but
when she believed it, she began to cry; she was not
pleased at the news.

"Well, I congratulate you," she said.   "But
why is it so sudden?"

"No, it's not sudden.   It's been going on since
March, only you don't notice anything. . . . I fell
in love with her last March when I made her acquaintance here, in your rooms."

"I thought you would marry some one in our
Moscow set," said Nina Fyodorovna after a pause.
"Girls in our set are simpler.   But what matters,
Alyosha, is that you should be happy — that matters most.   My Grigory Nikolaitch did not love me,
and there's no concealing it; you can see what our
life is.   Of course any woman may love you for
your goodness and your brains, but, you see, Yulitchka is a girl of good family from a high-class
boarding-school; goodness and brains are not enough
for her.   She is young, and, you, Alyosha, are not
so young, and are not good-looking."

To soften the last words, she stroked his head and
said:

"You're not good-looking, but you're a dear."

She was so agitated that a faint flush came into
her cheeks, and she began discussing eagerly whether
it would be the proper thing for her to bless Alyosha
with the ikon at the wedding.   She was, she rea-

soned, his elder sister, and took the place of his
mother; and she kept trying to convince her dejected
brother that the wedding must be celebrated in
proper style, with pomp and gaiety, so that no one
could find fault with it.

Then he began going to the Byelavins' as an accepted suitor, three or four times a day; and now
he never had time to take Sasha's place and read
aloud the historical novel.   Yulia used to receive
him in her two rooms, which were at a distance from
the drawing-room and her father's study, and he
liked them very much.   The walls in them were
dark; in the corner stood a case of ikons; and there
was a smell of good scent and of the oil in the holy
lamp.   Her rooms were at the furthest end of the
house; her bedstead and dressing-table were shut off
by a screen.   The doors of the bookcase were covered on the inside with a green curtain, and there
were rugs on the floor, so that her footsteps were
noiseless — and from this he concluded that she was
of a reserved character, and that she liked a quiet,
peaceful, secluded life.   In her own home she was
treated as though she were not quite grown up.   She
had no money of her own, and sometimes when they
were out for walks together, she was overcome with
confusion at not having a farthing.   Her father allowed her very little for dress and books, hardly
ten pounds a year.   And, indeed, the doctor himself
had not much money in spite of his good practice.
He played cards every night at the club, and always

lost. Moreover, he bought mortgaged houses through a building society, and let them. The tenants were irregular in paying the rent, but he was convinced that such speculations were profitable. He had mortgaged his own house in which he and his daughter were living, and with the money so raised had bought a piece of waste ground, and had already begun to build on it a large two-storey house, meaning to mortgage it, too, as soon as it was finished.

Laptev now lived in a sort of cloud, feeling as though he were not himself, but his double, and did many things which he would never have brought himself to do before. He went three or four times to the club with the doctor, had supper with him, and offered him money for house-building. He even visited Panaurov at his other establishment. It somehow happened that Panaurov invited him to dinner, and without thinking, Laptev accepted. He was received by a lady of five-and-thirty. She was tall and thin, with hair touched with grey, and black eyebrows, apparently not Russian. There were white patches of powder on her face. She gave him a honeyed smile and pressed his hand jerkily, so that the bracelets on her white hands tinkled. It seemed to Laptev that she smiled like that because she wanted to conceal from herself and from others that she was unhappy. He also saw two little girls, aged five and three, who had a marked likeness to Sasha. For dinner they had milk-soup, cold veal, and chocolate.   It was insipid and not good; but the table was splendid, with gold forks, bottles of Soyer, and cayenne pepper, an extraordinary bizarre cruet-stand, and a gold pepper-pot.

It was only as he was finishing the milk-soup that Laptev realised how very inappropriate it was for him to be dining there.   The lady was embarrassed, and kept smiling, showing her teeth.   Panaurov expounded didactically what being in love was, and what it was due to.

"We have in it an example of the action of electricity," he said in French, addressing the lady. "Every man has in his skin microscopic glands which contain currents of electricity.   If you meet with a person whose currents are parallel with your own, then you get love."

When Laptev went home and his sister asked him where he had been he felt awkward, and made no answer.

He felt himself in a false position right up to the time of the wedding.   His love grew more intense every day, and Yulia seemed to him a poetic and exalted creature; but, all the same, there was no mutual love, and the truth was that he was buying her and she was selling herself.   Sometimes, thinking things over, he fell into despair and asked himself: should he run away?   He did not sleep for nights together, and kept thinking how he should meet in Moscow the lady whom he had called in his letters " a certain person," and what attitude his father and his brother, difficult people, would take towards his marriage and towards Yulia. He was afraid that his father would say something rude to Yulia at their first meeting. And something strange had happened of late to his brother Fyodor. In his long letters he had taken to writing of the importance of health, of the effect of illness on the mental condition, of the meaning of religion, but not a word about Moscow or business. These letters irritated Laptev, and he thought his brother's character was changing for the worse.

The wedding was in September. The ceremony took place at the Church of St. Peter and St. Paul, after mass, and the same day the young couple set off for Moscow. When Laptev and his wife, in a black dress with a long train, already looking not a girl but a married woman, said good-bye to Nina Fyodorovna, the invalid's face worked, but there was no tear in her dry eyes. She said:

"If — which God forbid — I should die, take care of my little girls."

"Oh, I promise!" answered Yulia Sergeyevna, and her lips and eyelids began quivering too.

"I shall come to see you in October," said Laptev, much moved. "You must get better, my darling."

They travelled in a special compartment. Both felt depressed and uncomfortable. She sat in the corner without taking off her hat, and made a show of dozing, and he lay on the seat opposite, and he was disturbed by various thoughts — of his father, of " a certain person," whether Yulia would like her Moscow flat.   And looking at his wife, who did not love him, he wondered dejectedly " why this had happened."

V

The Laptevs had a wholesale business in Moscow, dealing in fancy goods: fringe, tape, trimmings, crochet cotton, buttons, and so on.   The gross receipts reached two millions a year; what the net profit was, no one knew but the old father.   The sons and the clerks estimated the profits at approximately three hundred thousand, and said that it would have been a hundred thousand more if the old man had not " been too free-handed "— that is, had not allowed credit indiscriminately.   In the last ten years alone the bad debts had mounted up to the sum of a million; and when the subject was referred to, the senior clerk would wink slyly and deliver himself of sentences the meaning of which was not clear to every one:

" The psychological sequences of the age."

Their chief commercial operations were conducted in the town market in a building which was called the warehouse.   The entrance to the warehouse was in the yard, where it was always dark, and smelt of matting and where the dray-horses were always stamping their hoofs on the asphalt.   A very humble-looking door, studded with iron, led from the

yard into a room with walls discoloured by damp
and scrawled over with charcoal, lighted up by a
narrow window covered by an iron grating. Then
on the left was another room larger and cleaner with
an iron stove and a couple of chairs, though it, too,
had a prison window: this was the office, and from
it a narrow stone staircase led up to the second
storey, where the principal room was. This was
rather a large room, but owing to the perpetual darkness, the low-pitched ceiling, the piles of boxes and
bales, and the numbers of men that kept flitting to
and fro in it, it made as unpleasant an impression on
a newcomer as the others. In the offices on the top
storey the goods lay in bales, in bundles and in card-
board boxes on the shelves; there was no order nor
neatness in the arrangement of it, and if crimson
threads, tassels, ends of fringe, had not peeped out
here and there from holes in the paper parcels, no
one could have guessed what was being bought and
sold here. And looking at these crumpled paper
parcels and boxes, no one would have believed that
a million was being made out of such trash, and
that fifty men were employed every day in this warehouse, not counting the buyers.

When at midday, on the day after his arrival at
Moscow, Laptev went into the warehouse, the workmen packing the goods were hammering so loudly
that in the outer room and the office no one heard
him come in. A postman he knew was coming down
the stairs with a bundle of letters in his hand; he

was wincing at the noise, and he did not notice Laptev either.   The first person to meet him upstairs was his brother Fyodor Fyodorovitch, who was so like him that they passed for twins.   This resemblance always reminded Laptev of his own personal appearance, and now, seeing before him a short, red-faced man with rather thin hair, with narrow plebeian hips, looking so uninteresting and so unintellectual, he asked himself:

" Can I really look like that? "

" How glad I am to see you! " said Fyodor, kissing his brother and pressing his hand warmly.   " I have been impatiently looking forward to seeing you every day, my dear fellow.   When you wrote that you were getting married, I was tormented with curiosity, and I've missed you, too, brother.   Only fancy, it's six months since we saw each other.   Well?   How goes it?   Nina's very bad?   Awfully bad? "

" Awfully bad."

" It's in God's hands," sighed Fyodor.   " Well, what of your wife?   She's a beauty, no doubt?   I love her already.   Of course, she is my little sister now.   We'll make much of her between us."

Laptev saw the broad, bent back — so familiar to him — of his father, Fyodor Stepanovitch.   The old man was sitting on a stool near the counter, talking to a customer.

" Father, God has sent us joy! " cried Fyodor. " Brother has come! "

Fyodor Stepanovitch was a tall man of exceptionally powerful build, so that, in spite of his wrinkles
and eighty years, he still looked a hale and vigorous man.   He spoke in a deep, rich, sonorous voice,
that resounded from his broad chest as from a barrel.   He wore no beard, but a short-clipped military moustache, and smoked cigars.   As he was
always too hot, he used all the year round to wear
a canvas coat at home and at the warehouse.   He
had lately had an operation for cataract.   His sight
was bad, and he did nothing in the business but talk
to the customers and have tea and jam with
them.

Laptev bent down and kissed his head and then
his lips.

" It's a good long time since we saw you, hon-
oured sir," said the old man —" a good long time.
Well, am I to congratulate you on entering the state
of holy matrimony?   Very well, then; I congratulate you."

And he put his lips out to be kissed.   Laptev bent
down and kissed him.

" Well, have you brought your young lady? " the
old man asked, and without waiting for an answer,
he said, addressing the customer: " ' Herewith I
beg to inform you, father, that I'm going to marry
such and such a young lady.'   Yes.   But as for asking for his father's counsel or blessing, that's not
in the rules nowadays.   Now they go their own
way.   When I married I was over forty, but I went

on my knees to my father and asked his advice. Nowadays we've none of that."

The old man was delighted to see his son, but thought it unseemly to show his affection or make any display of his joy. His voice and his manner of saying " your young lady " brought back to Laptev the depression he had always felt in the warehouse. Here every trifling detail reminded him of the past, when he used to be flogged and put on Lenten fare; he knew that even now boys were thrashed and punched in the face till their noses bled, and that when those boys grew up they would beat others. And before he had been five minutes in the warehouse, he always felt as though he were being scolded or punched in the face.

Fyodor slapped the customer on the shoulder and said to his brother:

" Here, Alyosha, I must introduce our Tambov benefactor, Grigory Timofeitch. He might serve as an example for the young men of the day; he's passed his fiftieth birthday, and he has tiny children."

The clerks laughed, and the customer, a lean old man with a pale face, laughed too.

" Nature above the normal capacity," observed the head-clerk, who was standing at the counter close by. " It always comes out when it's there."

The head-clerk — a tall man of fifty, in spectacles, with a dark beard, and a pencil behind his ear — usually expressed his ideas vaguely in roundabout

hints, while his sly smile betrayed that he attached
particular significance to his words. He liked to
obscure his utterances with bookish words, which he
understood in his own way, and many such words
he used in a wrong sense. For instance, the word
" except." When he had expressed some opinion
positively and did not want to be contradicted, he
would stretch out his hand and pronounce:

" Except! "

And what was most astonishing, the customers
and the other clerks understood him perfectly.
His name was Ivan Vassilitch Potchatkin, and he
came from Kashira. Now, congratulating Laptev,
he expressed himself as follows:

" It's the reward of valour, for the female heart
is a strong opponent."

Another important person in the warehouse was
a clerk called Makeitchev — a stout, solid, fair man
with whiskers and a perfectly bald head. He went
up to Laptev and congratulated him respectfully in
a low voice:

" I have the honour, sir. . . . The Lord has
heard your parent's prayer. Thank God."

Then the other clerks began coming up to congratulate him on his marriage. They were all fashionably dressed, and looked like perfectly well-bred,
educated men. Since between every two words they
put in a " sir," their congratulations — something
like " Best wishes, sir, for happiness, sir," uttered
very rapidly in a low voice — sounded rather like

the hiss of a whip in the air —" Shshsh-s s s s s! "

Laptev was soon bored and longing to go home, but it was awkward to go away. He was obliged to stay at least two hours at the warehouse to keep up appearances. He walked away from the counter and began asking Makeitchev whether things had gone well while he was away, and whether anything new had turned up, and the clerk answered him respectfully, avoiding his eyes. A boy with a cropped head, wearing a grey blouse, handed Laptev a glass of tea without a saucer; not long afterwards another boy, passing by, stumbled over a box, and almost fell down, and Makeitchev's face looked suddenly spiteful and ferocious like a wild beast's, and he shouted at him:

" Keep on your feet! "

The clerks were pleased that their young master was married and had come back at last; they looked at him with curiosity and friendly feeling, and each one thought it his duty to say something agreeable when he passed him. But Laptev was convinced that it was not genuine, and that they were only flattering him because they were afraid of him. He never could forget how fifteen years before, a clerk, who was mentally deranged, had run out into the street with nothing on but his shirt and shaking his fists at the windows, shouted that he had been ill-treated; and how, when the poor fellow had recovered, the clerks had jeered at him for long afterwards, reminding him how he had called his

employers "planters" instead of "exploiters."
Altogether the employés at Laptevs' had a very
poor time of it, and this fact was a subject of conversation for the whole market. The worst of it
was that the old man, Fyodor Stepanovitch, maintained something of an Asiatic despotism in his attitude to them. Thus, no one knew what wages
were paid to the old man's favourites, Potchatkin
and Makeitchev. They received no more than
three thousand a year, together with bonuses, but
he made out that he paid then seven. The bonuses
were given to all the clerks every year, but privately,
so that the man who got little was bound from vanity to say he had got more. Not one boy knew
when he would be promoted to be a clerk; not one
of the men knew whether his employer was satisfied with him or not. Nothing was directly forbidden, and so the clerks never knew what was allowed,
and what was not. They were not forbidden to
marry, but they did not marry for fear of displeas-
ing their employer and losing their place. They
were allowed to have friends and pay visits, but
the gates were shut at nine o'clock, and every morning the old man scanned them all suspiciously, and
tried to detect any smell of vodka about them:
" Now then, breathe," he would say.

Every clerk was obliged to go to early service,
and to stand in church in such a position that the
old man could see them all. The fasts were strictly
observed. On great occasions, such as the birth-

day of their employer or of any member of his family, the clerks had to subscribe and present a cake
from Fley's, or an album.   The clerks lived three
or four in a room in the lower storey, and in the
lodges of the house in Pyatnitsky Street, and at
dinner ate from a common bowl, though there was
a plate set before each of them.   If one of the family came into the room while they were at dinner,
they all stood up.

Laptev was conscious that only, perhaps, those
among them who had been corrupted by the old
man's training could seriously regard him as their
benefactor; the others must have looked on him as
an enemy and a " planter."   Now, after six months'
absence, he saw no change for the better; there was
indeed something new which boded nothing good.
His brother Fyodor, who had always been quiet,
thoughtful, and extremely refined, was now running
about the warehouse with a pencil behind his ear
making a show of being very busy and business-
like, slapping customers on the shoulder and shouting " Friends! " to the clerks.   Apparently he had
taken up a new rôle, and Alexey did not recognise
him in the part.

The old man's voice boomed unceasingly.   Having nothing to do, he was laying down the law to
a customer, telling him how he should order his life
and his business, always holding himself up as an
example.   That boastfulness, that aggressive tone
of authority, Laptev had heard ten, fifteen, twenty

years ago. The old man adored himself; from what he said it always appeared that he had made his wife and all her relations happy, that he had been munificent to his children, and a benefactor to his clerks and employés, and that every one in the street and all his acquaintances remembered him in their prayers. Whatever he did was always right, and if things went wrong with people it was because they did not take his advice; without his advice nothing could succeed. In church he stood in the foremost place, and even made observations to the priests, if in his opinion they were not conducting the service properly, and believed that this was pleasing God because God loved him.

At two o'clock every one in the warehouse was hard at work, except the old man, who still went on booming in his deep voice. To avoid standing idle, Laptev took some trimmings from a workgirl and let her go; then listened to a customer, a merchant from Vologda, and told a clerk to attend to him.

" T. V. A. ! " resounded on all sides (prices were denoted by letters in the warehouse and goods by numbers). " R. I. T. ! " As he went away, Laptev said good-bye to no one but Fyodor.

" I shall come to Pyatnitsky Street with my wife to-morrow," he said; " but I warn you, if father says a single rude thing to her, I shall not stay there another minute."

" You're the same as ever," sighed Fyodor. " Marriage has not changed you. You must be pa-

tient with the old man.   So till eleven o'clock, then.
We shall expect you impatiently.   Come directly
after mass, then."

"I don't go to mass."

"That does not matter.   The great thing is not
to be later than eleven, so you may be in time to
pray to God and to lunch with us.   Give my greetings to my little sister and kiss her hand for me.   I
have a presentiment that I shall like her," Fyodor
added with perfect sincerity.   "I envy you,
brother!" he shouted after him as Alexey went
downstairs.

"And why does he shrink into himself in that
shy way as though he fancied he was naked?"
thought Laptev, as he walked along Nikolsky
Street, trying to understand the change that had
come over his brother.   "And his language is new,
too: 'Brother, dear brother, God has sent us joy;
to pray to God'— just like Iudushka in Shtchedrin."

VI

At eleven o'clock the next day, which was Sunday, he was driving with his wife along Pyatnitsky
Street in a light, one-horse carriage.   He was
afraid of his father's doing something outrageous,
and was already ill at ease.   After two nights in
her husband's house Yulia Sergeyevna considered
her marriage a mistake and a calamity, and if she
had had to live with her husband in any other town
but Moscow, it seemed to her that she could not

have endured the horror of it. Moscow entertained her — she was delighted with the streets,
the churches; and if it had been possible to drive
about Moscow in those splendid sledges with expensive horses, to drive the whole day from morning
till night, and with the swift motion to feel the cold
autumn air blowing upon her, she would perhaps not
have felt herself so unhappy.

Near a white, lately stuccoed two-storey house
the coachman pulled up his horse, and began to turn
to the right. They were expected, and near the
gate stood two policemen and the porter in a new
full-skirted coat, high boots, and goloshes. The
whole space, from the middle of the street to the
gates and all over the yard from the porch, was
strewn with fresh sand. The porter took off his hat,
the policemen saluted. Near the entrance Fyodor
met them with a very serious face.

" Very glad to make your acquaintance, little sister," he said, kissing Yulia's hand. " You're very
welcome."

He led her upstairs on his arm, and then along
a corridor through a crowd of men and women.
The anteroom was crowded too, and smelt of incense.

" I will introduce you to our father directly,"
whispered Fyodor in the midst of a solemn, deathly
silence. " A venerable old man, *pater-familias*."

In the big drawing-room, by a table prepared for
service, Fyodor Stepanovitch stood, evidently wait-

ing for them, and with him the priest in a calotte, and a deacon.   The old man shook hands with Yulia without saying a word.   Every one was silent. Yulia was overcome with confusion.

The priest and the deacon began putting on their vestments.   A censer was brought in, giving off sparks and fumes of incense and charcoal.   The candles were lighted.   The clerks walked into the drawing-room on tiptoe and stood in two rows along the wall.   There was perfect stillness, no one even coughed.

"The blessing of God," began the deacon.

The service was read with great solemnity; nothing was left out and two canticles were sung — to sweetest Jesus and the most Holy Mother of God. The singers sang very slowly, holding up the music before them.   Laptev noticed how confused his wife was.   While they were singing the canticles, and the singers in different keys brought out "Lord have mercy on us," he kept expecting in nervous suspense that the old man would make some remark such as, "You don't know how to cross yourself," and he felt vexed.   Why this crowd, and why this ceremony with priests and choristers?   It was too bourgeois.   But when she, like the old man, put her head under the gospel and afterwards several times dropped upon her knees, he realised that she liked it all, and was reassured.

At the end of the service, during " Many, many

years," the priest gave the old man and Alexey the cross to kiss, but when Yulia went up, he put his hand over the cross, and showed he wanted to speak. Signs were made to the singers to stop.

" The prophet Samuel," began the priest, " went to Bethlehem at the bidding of the Lord, and there the elders of the town with fear and trembling asked him: ' Comest thou peaceably? ' And the prophet answered: ' Peaceably: I am come to sacrifice unto the Lord: sanctify yourselves and come with me to the sacrifice.' Even so, Yulia, servant of God, shall we ask of thee, Dost thou come bringing peace into this house? "

Yulia flushed with emotion. As he finished, the priest gave her the cross to kiss, and said in quite a different tone of voice:

" Now Fyodor Fyodorovitch must be married; it's high time."

The choir began singing once more, people began moving, and the room was noisy again. The old man, much touched, with his eyes full of tears, kissed Yulia three times, made the sign of the cross over her face, and said:

" This is your home. I'm an old man and need nothing."

The clerks congratulated her and said something, but the choir was singing so loud that nothing else could be heard. Then they had lunch and drank champagne. She sat beside the old father, and he talked to her, saying that families ought not to be parted but live together in one house; that separation and disunion led to permanent rupture.

" I've made money and the children only do the spending of it," he said.   " Now, you live with me and save money.   It's time for an old man like me to rest."

Yulia had all the time a vision of Fyodor flitting about so like her husband, but shyer and more restless; he fussed about her and often kissed her hand.

" We are plain people, little sister," he said, and patches of red came into his face as he spoke.   " We live simply in Russian style, like Christians, little sister."

As they went home, Laptev felt greatly relieved that everything had gone off so well, and that nothing outrageous had happened as he had expected. He said to his wife:

" You're surprised that such a stalwart, broad-shouldered father should have such stunted, narrow-chested sons as Fyodor and me.   Yes; but it's easy to explain!   My father married my mother when he was forty-five, and she was only seventeen. She turned pale and trembled in his presence.   Nina was born first — born of a comparatively healthy mother, and so she was finer and sturdier than we were.   Fyodor and I were begotten and born after mother had been worn out by terror.   I can remember my father correcting me — or, to speak plainly, beating me — before I was five years old.   He used to thrash me with a birch, pull my ears, hit me on the head, and every morning when I woke up my first thought was whether he would beat me that day. Play and childish mischief was forbidden us. We had to go to morning service and to early mass. When we met priests or monks we had to kiss their hands; at home we had to sing hymns. Here you are religious and love all that, but I'm afraid of religion, and when I pass a church I remember my childhood, and am overcome with horror. I was taken to the warehouse as soon as I was eight years old. I worked like a working boy, and it was bad for my health, for I used to be beaten there every day. Afterwards when I went to the high school, I used to go to school till dinner-time, and after dinner I had to sit in that warehouse till evening; and things went on like that till I was twenty-two, till I got to know Yartsev, and he persuaded me to leave my father's house. That Yartsev did a great deal for me. I tell you what," said Laptev, and he laughed with pleasure: " let us go and pay Yartsev a visit at once. He's a very fine fellow! How touched he will be! "

VII

On a Saturday in November Anton Rubinstein was conducting in a symphony concert. It was very hot and crowded. Laptev stood behind the columns, while his wife and Kostya Kotchevoy were sitting in the third or fourth row some distance in front.   At the very beginning of an interval a " certain person," Polina Nikolaevna Razsudin, quite unexpectedly passed by him. He had often since his marriage thought with trepidation of a possible meeting with her. When now she looked at him openly and directly, he realised that he had all this time shirked having things out with her, or writing her two or three friendly lines, as though he had been hiding from her; he felt ashamed and flushed crimson. She pressed his hand tightly and impulsively and asked:

" Have you seen Yartsev? "

And without waiting for an answer she went striding on impetuously as though some one were pushing her on from behind.

She was very thin and plain, with a long nose; her face always looked tired, and exhausted, and it seemed as though it were an effort to her to keep her eyes open, and not to fall down. She had fine, dark eyes, and an intelligent, kind, sincere expression, but her movements were awkward and abrupt. It was hard to talk to her, because she could not talk or listen quietly. Loving her was not easy. Sometimes when she was alone with Laptev she would go on laughing for a long time, hiding her face in her hands, and would declare that love was not the chief thing in life for her, and would be as whimsical as a girl of seventeen; and before kissing her he would have to put out all the candles. She was thirty. She was married to a schoolmaster, but had not lived with her husband for years. She earned her living by giving music lessons and playing in quartettes.

During the ninth symphony she passed again as though by accident, but the crowd of men standing like a thick wall behind the columns prevented her going further, and she remained beside him. Laptev saw that she was wearing the same little velvet blouse she had worn at concerts last year and the year before. Her gloves were new, and her fan, too, was new, but it was a common one. She was fond of fine clothes, but she did not know how to dress, and grudged spending money on it. She dressed so badly and untidily that when she was going to her lessons striding hurriedly down the street, she might easily have been taken for a young monk.

The public applauded and shouted encore.

" You'll spend the evening with me," said Polina Nikolaevna, going up to Laptev and looking at him severely. " When this is over we'll go and have tea. Do you hear? I insist on it. You owe me a great deal, and haven't the moral right to refuse me such a trifle."

" Very well; let us go," Laptev assented.

Endless calls followed the conclusion of the concert. The audience got up from their seats and went out very slowly, and Laptev could not go away without telling his wife. He had to stand at the door and wait.

"I'm dying for some tea," Polina Nikolaevna
said plaintively. "My very soul is parched."

"You can get something to drink here," said
Laptev. "Let's go to the buffet."

"Oh, I've no money to fling away on waiters.
I'm not a shopkeeper."

He offered her his arm; she refused, in a long,
wearisome sentence which he had heard many times,
to the effect that she did not class herself with the
feebler fair sex, and did not depend on the services
of gentlemen.

As she talked to him she kept looking about at
the audience and greeting acquaintances; they were
her fellow-students at the higher courses and at the
conservatorium, and her pupils. She gripped their
hands abruptly, as though she were tugging at them.
But then she began twitching her shoulders, and
trembling as though she were in a fever, and at last
said softly, looking at Laptev with horror:

"Who is it you've married? Where were your
eyes, you mad fellow? What did you see in that
stupid, insignificant girl? Why, I loved you for
your mind, for your soul, but that china doll wants
nothing but your money!"

"Let us drop that, Polina," he said in a voice of
supplication. "All that you can say to me about
my marriage I've said to myself many times already.
. . . Don't cause me unnecessary pain."

Yulia Sergeyevna made her appearance, wearing
a black dress with a big diamond brooch, which her

father-in-law had sent her after the service. She was followed by her suite — Kotchevoy, two doctors of their acquaintance, an officer, and a stout young man in student's uniform, called Kish.

" You go on with Kostya," Laptev said to his wife. " I'm coming later."

Yulia nodded and went on. Polina Nikolaevna gazed after her, quivering all over and twitching nervously, and in her eyes there was a look of repulsion, hatred, and pain.

Laptev was afraid to go home with her, foreseeing an unpleasant discussion, cutting words, and tears, and he suggested that they should go and have tea at a restaurant. But she said:

" No, no. I want to go home. Don't dare to talk to me of restaurants."

She did not like being in a restaurant, because the atmosphere of restaurants seemed to her poisoned by tobacco smoke and the breath of men. Against all men she did not know she cherished a strange prejudice, regarding them all as immoral rakes, capable of attacking her at any moment. Besides, the music played at restaurants jarred on her nerves and gave her a headache.

Coming out of the Hall of Nobility, they took a sledge in Ostozhenka and drove to Savelovsky Lane, where she lodged. All the way Laptev thought about her. It was true that he owed her a great deal. He had made her acquaintance at the flat of his friend Yartsev, to whom she was giving les-

sons in harmony.   Her love for him was deep and
perfectly disinterested, and her relations with him
did not alter her habits; she went on giving her lessons and wearing herself out with work as before.
Through her he came to understand and love music,
which he had scarcely cared for till then.

"Half my kingdom for a cup of tea!" she pronounced in a hollow voice, covering her mouth with
her muff that she might not catch cold.   "I've given
five lessons, confound them! My pupils are as
stupid as posts; I nearly died of exasperation.   I
don't know how long this slavery can go on.   I'm
worn out.   As soon as I can scrape together three
hundred roubles, I shall throw it all up and go to
the Crimea, to lie on the beach and drink in ozone.
How I love the sea — oh, how I love the sea!"

"You'll never go," said Laptev.   "To begin
with, you'll never save the money; and, besides, you'd
grudge spending it.   Forgive me, I repeat again:
surely it's quite as humiliating to collect the money
by farthings from idle people who have music lessons to while away their time, as to borrow it from
your friends."

"I haven't any friends," she said irritably.
"And please don't talk nonsense. The working
class to which I belong has one privilege: the consciousness of being incorruptible — the right to refuse to be indebted to wretched little shopkeepers,
and to treat them with scorn.   No, indeed, you don't
buy me! I'm not a Yulitchka!"

Laptev did not attempt to pay the driver, knowing that it would call forth a perfect torrent of words, such as he had often heard before. She paid herself.

She had a little furnished room in the flat of a solitary lady who provided her meals. Her big Becker piano was for the time at Yartsev's in Great Nikitsky Street, and she went there every day to play on it. In her room there were armchairs in loose covers, a bed with a white summer quilt, and flowers belonging to the landlady; there were oleographs on the walls, and there was nothing that would have suggested that there was a woman, and a woman of university education, living in it. There was no toilet table; there were no books; there was not even a writing-table. It was evident that she went to bed as soon as she got home, and went out as soon as she got up in the morning.

The cook brought in the samovar. Polina Nikolaevna made tea, and, still shivering — the room was cold — began abusing the singers who had sung in the ninth symphony. She was so tired she could hardly keep her eyes open. She drank one glass of tea, then a second, and then a third.

" And so you are married," she said. " But don't be uneasy; I'm not going to pine away. I shall be able to tear you out of my heart. Only it's annoying and bitter to me that you are just as contemptible as every one else; that what you want in a woman is not brains or intellect, but simply a body, good looks, and youth. . . . Youth!" she pronounced through her nose, as though mimicking some one, and she laughed. "Youth! You must have purity, *reinheit! reinheit!*" she laughed, throwing herself back in her chair. "*Reinheit!*"

When she left off laughing her eyes were wet with tears.

"You're happy, at any rate?" she asked.

"No."

"Does she love you?"

"No."

Laptev, agitated, and feeling miserable, stood up and began walking about the room.

"No," he repeated. "If you want to know, Polina, I'm very unhappy. There's no help for it; I've done the stupid thing, and there's no correcting it now. I must look at it philosophically. She married me without love, stupidly, perhaps with mercenary motives, but without understanding, and now she evidently sees her mistake and is miserable. I see it. At night we sleep together, but by day she is afraid to be left alone with me for five minutes, and tries to find distraction, society. With me she feels ashamed and frightened."

"And yet she takes money from you?"

"That's stupid, Polina!" cried Laptev. "She takes money from me because it makes absolutely no difference to her whether she has it or not. She is an honest, pure girl. She married me simply because she wanted to get away from her father, that's all."

" And are you sure she would have married you if you had not been rich? " asked Polina.

" I'm not sure of anything," said Laptev dejectedly. " Not of anything. I don't understand anything. For God's sake, Polina, don't let us talk about it."

" Do you love her? "

" Desperately."

A silence followed. She drank a fourth glass, while he paced up and down, thinking that by now his wife was probably having supper at the doctors' club.

" But is it possible to love without knowing why? " asked Polina, shrugging her shoulders. " No; it's the promptings of animal passion! You are poisoned, intoxicated by that beautiful body, that *reinheit!* Go away from me; you are unclean! Go to her! "

She brandished her hand at him, then took up his hat and hurled it at him. He put on his fur coat without speaking and went out, but she ran after him into the passage, clutched his arm above the elbow, and broke into sobs.

" Hush, Polina! Don't! " he said, and could not unclasp her fingers. " Calm yourself, I entreat you."

She shut her eyes and turned pale, and her long

nose became an unpleasant waxy colour like a
corpse's, and Laptev still could not unclasp her fingers. She had fainted. He lifted her up carefully, laid her on her bed, and sat by her for ten minutes till she came to herself. Her hands were cold,
her pulse was weak and uneven.

"Go home," she said, opening her eyes. "Go
away, or I shall begin howling again. I must take
myself in hand."

When he came out, instead of going to the doctors' club where his friends were expecting him, he
went home. All the way home he was asking himself reproachfully why he had not settled down to
married life with that woman who loved him so
much, and was in reality his wife and friend. She
was the one human being who was devoted to him;
and, besides, would it not have been a grateful and
worthy task to give happiness, peace, and a home
to that proud, clever, overworked creature? Was
it for him, he asked himself, to lay claim to youth
and beauty, to that happiness which could not be,
and which, as though in punishment or mockery, had
kept him for the last three months in a state of
gloom and oppression. The honeymoon was long
over, and he still, absurd to say, did not know what
sort of person his wife was. To her school friends
and her father she wrote long letters of five sheets,
and was never at a loss for something to say to
them, but to him she never spoke except about the
weather or to tell him that dinner was ready, or

that it was supper-time. When at night she said her lengthy prayers and then kissed her crosses and ikons, he thought, watching her with hatred, "Here she's praying. What's she praying about? What about?" In his thoughts he showered insults on himself and her, telling himself that when he got into bed and took her into his arms, he was taking what he had paid for; but it was horrible. If only it had been a healthy, reckless, sinful woman; but here he had youth, piety, meekness, the pure eyes of innocence. . . . While they were engaged her piety had touched him; now the conventional definiteness of her views and convictions seemed to him a barrier, behind which the real truth could not be seen. Already everything in his married life was agonising. When his wife, sitting beside him in the theatre, sighed or laughed spontaneously, it was bitter to him that she enjoyed herself alone and would not share her delight with him. And it was remarkable that she was friendly with all his friends, and they all knew what she was like already, while he knew nothing about her, and only moped and was dumbly jealous.

When he got home Laptev put on his dressing-gown and slippers, and sat down in his study to read a novel. His wife was not at home. But within half an hour there was a ring at the hall door, and he heard the muffled footsteps of Pyotr running to open it. It was Yulia. She walked into the study in her fur coat, her cheeks rosy with the frost.

"There's a great fire in Pryesnya," she said breathlessly. "There's a tremendous glow. I'm going to see it with Konstantin Ivanovitch."

"Well, do, dear!"

The sight of her health, her freshness, and the childish horror in her eyes, reassured Laptev. He read for another half-hour and went to bed.

Next day Polina Nikolaevna sent to the warehouse two books she had borrowed from him, all his letters and his photographs; with them was a note consisting of one word —"*basta.*"

VIII

Towards the end of October Nina Fyodorovna had unmistakable symptoms of a relapse. There was a change in her face, and she grew rapidly thinner. In spite of acute pain she still imagined that she was getting better, and got up and dressed every morning as though she were well, and then lay on her bed, fully dressed, for the rest of the day. And towards the end she became very talkative. She would lie on her back and talk in a low voice, speaking with an effort and breathing painfully. She died suddenly under the following circumstances.

It was a clear moonlight evening. In the street people were tobogganing in the fresh snow, and their clamour floated in at the window. Nina Fyodorovna was lying on her back in bed, and Sasha, who had no one to take turns with her now, was sitting beside her half asleep.

"I don't remember his father's name," Nina Fyodorovna was saying softly, "but his name was Ivan Kotchevoy — a poor clerk. He was a sad drunkard, the Kingdom of Heaven be his! He used to come to us, and every month we used to give him a pound of sugar and two ounces of tea. And money, too, sometimes, of course. Yes. . . . And then, this is what happened. Our Kotchevoy began drinking heavily and died, consumed by vodka. He left a little son, a boy of seven. Poor little orphan! . . . We took him and hid him in the clerk's quarters, and he lived there for a whole year, without father's knowing. And when father did see him, he only waved his hand and said nothing. When Kostya, the little orphan, was nine years old — by that time I was engaged to be married — I took him round to all the day schools. I went from one to the other, and no one would take him. And he cried. . . . 'What are you crying for, little silly?' I said. I took him to Razgulyay to the second school, where — God bless them for it! — they took him, and the boy began going every day on foot from Pyatnitsky Street to Razgulyay Street and back again. . . . Alyosha paid for him. . . . By God's grace the boy got on, was good at his lessons, and turned out well. . . . He's a lawyer now in Moscow, a friend of Alyosha's, and so good in science. Yes, we had compassion on a fellow-creature and took him into our house, and now I daresay, he remembers us in his prayers. . . . Yes. . . ."

Nina Fyodorovna spoke more and more slowly
with long pauses, then after a brief silence she suddenly raised herself and sat up.

"There's something the matter with me . . .
something seems wrong," she said.   "Lord have
mercy on me!   Oh, I can't breathe!"

Sasha knew that her mother would soon die; seeing now how suddenly her face looked drawn, she
guessed that it was the end, and she was frightened.

"Mother, you mustn't!" she began sobbing.
"You mustn't."

"Run to the kitchen; let them go for father.   I
am very ill indeed."

Sasha ran through all the rooms calling, but there
were none of the servants in the house, and the only
person she found was Lida asleep on a chest in the
dining-room with her clothes on and without a pillow.   Sasha ran into the yard just as she was without her goloshes, and then into the street.   On a
bench at the gate her nurse was sitting watching the
tobogganing.   From beyond the river, where the
tobogganing slope was, came the strains of a military
band.

"Nurse, mother's dying!" sobbed Sasha.   "You
must go for father! . . ."

The nurse went upstairs, and, glancing at the sick
woman, thrust a lighted wax candle into her hand.
Sasha rushed about in terror and besought some
one to go for her father, then she put on a coat

and a kerchief, and ran into the street. From the
servants she knew already that her father had another wife and two children with whom he lived
in Bazarny Street. She ran out of the gate and
turned to the left, crying, and frightened of unknown
people. She soon began to sink into the snow and
grew numb with cold.

She met an empty sledge, but she did not take
it: perhaps, she thought, the man would drive her
out of town, rob her, and throw her into the cemetery (the servants had talked of such a case at tea).
She went on and on, sobbing and panting with ex-
haustion. When she got into Bazarny Street, she
inquired where M. Panaurov lived. An unknown
woman spent a long time directing her, and seeing
that she did not understand, took her by the hand
and led her to a house of one storey that stood
back from the street. The door stood open. Sasha
ran through the entry, along the corridor, and found
herself at last in a warm, lighted room where her
father was sitting by the samovar with a lady and
two children. But by now she was unable to utter a
word, and could only sob. Panaurov understood.

" Mother's worse? " he asked. " Tell me, child:
is mother worse? "

He was alarmed and sent for a sledge.

When they got home, Nina Fyodorovna was sitting propped up with pillows, with a candle in her
hand. Her face looked dark and her eyes were
closed. Crowding in the doorway stood the nurse,

the cook, the housemaid, a peasant called Prokofy and a few persons of the humbler class, who were complete strangers. The nurse was giving them orders in a whisper, and they did not understand. Inside the room at the window stood Lida, with a pale and sleepy face, gazing severely at her mother.

Panaurov took the candle out of Nina Fyodorovna's hand, and, frowning contemptuously, flung it on the chest of drawers.

"This is awful!" he said, and his shoulders quivered. "Nina, you must lie down," he said affectionately. "Lie down, dear."

She looked at him, but did not know him. . . . They laid her down on her back.

When the priest and the doctor, Sergey Borisovitch, arrived, the servants crossed themselves devoutly and prayed for her.

"What a sad business!" said the doctor thoughtfully, coming out into the drawing-room. "Why, she was still young — not yet forty."

They heard the loud sobbing of the little girls. Panaurov, with a pale face and moist eyes, went up to the doctor and said in a faint, weak voice:

"Do me a favour, my dear fellow. Send a telegram to Moscow. I'm not equal to it."

The doctor fetched the ink and wrote the following telegram to his daughter:

"Madame Panaurov died at eight o'clock this evening. Tell your husband: a mortgaged house for

sale in Dvoryansky Street, nine thousand cash.
Auction on twelfth. Advise him not miss opportunity."

IX

Laptev lived in one of the turnings out of Little
Dmitrovka. Besides the big house facing the street,
he rented also a two-storey lodge in the yard at the
back of his friend Kotchevoy, a lawyer's assistant
whom all the Laptevs called Kostya, because he had
grown up under their eyes. Facing this lodge stood
another, also of two storeys, inhabited by a French
family consisting of a husband and wife and five
daughters.

There was a frost of twenty degrees. The windows were frozen over. Waking up in the morning, Kostya, with an anxious face, took twenty drops
of a medicine; then, taking two dumb-bells out of
the bookcase, he did gymnastic exercises. He was
tall and thin, with big reddish moustaches; but what
was most noticeable in his appearance was the length
of his legs.

Pyotr, a middle-aged peasant in a reefer jacket
and cotton breeches tucked into his high boots,
brought in the samovar and made the tea.

" It's very nice weather now, Konstantin Ivanovitch," he said.

" It is, but I tell you what, brother, it's a pity we
can't get on, you and I, without such exclamations."

Pyotr sighed from politeness.

"What are the little girls doing?" asked Kotchevoy.

"The priest has not come. Alexey Fyodorovitch is giving them their lesson himself."

Kostya found a spot in the window that was not covered with frost, and began looking through a field-glass at the windows of the house where the French family lived.

"There's no seeing," he said.

Meanwhile Alexey Fyodorovitch was giving Sasha and Lida a scripture lesson below. For the last six weeks they had been living in Moscow, and were installed with their governess in the lower storey of the lodge. And three times a week a teacher from a school in the town, and a priest, came to give them lessons. Sasha was going through the New Testament and Lida was going through the Old. The time before Lida had been set the story up to Abraham to learn by heart.

"And so Adam and Eve had two sons," said Laptev. "Very good. But what were they called? Try to remember them!"

Lida, still with the same severe face, gazed dumbly at the table. She moved her lips, but without speaking; and the elder girl, Sasha, looked into her face, frowning.

"You know it very well, only you mustn't be nervous," said Laptev. "Come, what were Adam's sons called?"

"Abel and Canel," Lida whispered.

" Cain and Abel," Laptev corrected her.

A big tear rolled down Lida's cheek and dropped on the book. Sasha looked down and turned red, and she, too, was on the point of tears. Laptev felt a lump in his throat, and was so sorry for them he could not speak. He got up from the table and lighted a cigarette. At that moment Kotchevoy came down the stairs with a paper in his hand. The little girls stood up, and without looking at him, made curtsies.

" For God's sake, Kostya, give them their lessons," said Laptev, turning to him. " I'm afraid I shall cry, too, and I have to go to the warehouse before dinner."

" All right."

Alexey Fyodorovitch went away. Kostya, with a very serious face, sat down to the table and drew the Scripture history towards him.

" Well," he said; " where have you got to? "

" She knows about the Flood," said Sasha.

" The Flood? All right. Let's peg in at the Flood. Fire away about the Flood." Kostya skimmed through a brief description of the Flood in the book, and said: " I must remark that there really never was a flood such as is described here. And there was no such person as Noah. Some thousands of years before the birth of Christ, there was an extraordinary inundation of the earth, and that's not only mentioned in the Jewish Bible, but in the books of other ancient peoples: the Greeks, the

Chaldeans, the Hindoos.   But whatever the inundation may have been, it couldn't have covered the
whole earth.   It may have flooded the plains, but
the mountains must have remained.   You can read
this book, of course, but don't put too much faith
in it."

Tears trickled down Lida's face again.   She
turned away and suddenly burst into such loud sobs,
that Kostya started and jumped up from his seat in
great confusion.

" I want to go home," she said, " to papa and to
nurse."

Sasha cried too.   Kostya went upstairs to his own
room, and spoke on the telephone to Yulia Sergeyevna.

" My dear soul," he said, " the little girls are crying again; there's no doing anything with them."

Yulia Sergeyevna ran across from the big house
in her indoor dress, with only a knitted shawl over
her shoulders, and chilled through by the frost, began comforting the children.

" Do believe me, do believe me," she said in an
imploring voice, hugging first one and then the other.
" Your papa's coming to-day; he has sent a telegram.   You're grieving for mother, and I grieve
too.   My heart's torn, but what can we do?   We
must bow to God's will! "

When they left off crying, she wrapped them up
and took them out for a drive.   They stopped near
the Iverskoy chapel, put up candles at the shrine,

and, kneeling down, prayed. On the way back they went in Filippov's, and had cakes sprinkled with poppy-seeds.

The Laptevs had dinner between two and three. Pyotr handed the dishes. This Pyotr waited on the family, and by day ran to the post, to the warehouse, to the law courts for Kostya; he spent his evenings making cigarettes, ran to open the door at night, and before five o'clock in the morning was up lighting the stoves, and no one knew where he slept. He was very fond of opening seltzer-water bottles and did it easily, without a bang and without spilling a drop.

" With God's blessing," said Kostya, drinking off a glass of vodka before the soup.

At first Yulia Sergeyevna did not like Kostya; his bass voice, his phrases such as " Landed him one on the beak," " filth," " produce the samovar," etc., his habit of clinking glasses and making sentimental speeches, seemed to her trivial. But as she got to know him better, she began to feel very much at home with him. He was open with her; he liked talking to her in a low voice in the evening, and even gave her novels of his own composition to read, though these had been kept a secret even from such friends as Laptev and Yartsev. She read these novels and praised them, so that she might not disappoint him, and he was delighted because he hoped sooner or lated to become a distinguished author.

In his novels he described nothing but country-house life, though he had only seen the country on rare occasions when visiting friends at a summer villa, and had only been in a real country-house once in his life, when he had been to Volokolamsk on law business. He avoided any love interest as though he were ashamed of it; he put in frequent descriptions of nature, and in them was fond of using such expressions as, "the capricious lines of the mountains, the miraculous forms of the clouds, the harmony of mysterious rhythms. . . ." His novels had never been published, and this he attributed to the censorship.

He liked the duties of a lawyer, but yet he considered that his most important pursuit was not the law but these novels. He believed that he had a subtle, æsthetic temperament, and he always had leanings towards art. He neither sang nor played on any musical instrument, and was absolutely without an ear for music, but he attended all the symphony and philharmonic concerts, got up concerts for charitable objects, and made the acquaintance of singers. . . .

They used to talk at dinner.

"It's a strange thing," said Laptev, "my Fyodor took my breath away again! He said we must find out the date of the centenary of our firm, so as to try and get raised to noble rank; and he said it quite seriously. What can be the matter with him? I confess I begin to feel worried about him."

They talked of Fyodor, and of its being the fashion nowadays to adopt some pose or other. Fyodor, for instance, tried to appear like a plain merchant, though he had ceased to be one; and when the teacher came from the school, of which old Laptev was the patron, to ask Fyodor for his salary, the latter changed his voice and deportment, and behaved with the teacher as though he were some one in authority.

There was nothing to be done; after dinner they went into the study. They talked about the decadents, about "The Maid of Orleans," and Kostya delivered a regular monologue; he fancied that he was very successful in imitating Ermolova. Then they sat down and played whist. The little girls had not gone back to the lodge but were sitting together in one arm-chair, with pale and mournful faces, and were listening to every noise in the street, wondering whether it was their father coming. In the evening when it was dark and the candles were lighted, they felt deeply dejected. The talk over the whist, the footsteps of Pyotr, the crackling in the fireplace, jarred on their nerves, and they did not like to look at the fire. In the evenings they did not want to cry, but they felt strange, and there was a load on their hearts. They could not understand how people could talk and laugh when their mother was dead.

"What did you see through the field-glasses today?" Yulia Sergeyevna asked Kostya.

"Nothing to-day, but yesterday I saw the old Frenchman having his bath."

At seven o'clock Yulia and Kostya went to the Little Theatre. Laptev was left with the little girls.

"It's time your father was here," he said, looking at his watch. "The train must be late."

The children sat in their arm-chair dumb and huddling together like animals when they are cold, while he walked about the room looking impatiently at his watch. It was quiet in the house. But just before nine o'clock some one rang at the bell. Pyotr went to open the door.

Hearing a familiar voice, the children shrieked, burst into sobs, and ran into the hall. Panaurov was wearing a sumptuous coat of antelope skin, and his head and moustaches were white with hoar frost. "In a minute, in a minute," he muttered, while Sasha and Lida, sobbing and laughing, kissed his cold hands, his hat, his antelope coat. With the languor of a handsome man spoilt by too much love, he fondled the children without haste, then went into the study and said, rubbing his hands:

"I've not come to stay long, my friends. I'm going to Petersburg to-morrow. They've promised to transfer me to another town."

He was staying at the Dresden Hotel.

X

A friend who was often at the Laptevs' was Ivan Gavrilitch Yartsev. He was a strong, healthy man with black hair and a clever, pleasant face. He was considered to be handsome, but of late he had begun to grow stout, and that rather spoilt his face and figure; another thing that spoilt him was that he wore his hair cut so close that the skin showed through.

At the University his tall figure and physical strength had won him the nickname of "the pounder" among the students. He had taken his degree with the Laptev brothers in the faculty of philology — then he went in for science and now had the degree of *magister* in chemistry. But he had never given a lecture or even been a demonstrator. He taught physics and natural history in the modern school, and in two girls' high schools. He was enthusiastic over his pupils, especially the girls, and used to maintain that a remarkable generation was growing up. At home he spent his time studying sociology and Russian history, as well as chemistry, and he sometimes published brief notes in the newspapers and magazines, signing them " Y." When he talked of some botanical or zoological subject, he spoke like an historian; when he was discussing some historical question, he approached it as a man of science.

Kish, nicknamed " the eternal student," was also

like one of the family at the Laptevs'.   He had been
for three years studying medicine.   Then he took
up mathematics, and spent two years over each
year's course.   His father, a provincial druggist,
used to send him forty roubles a month, to which
his mother, without his father's knowledge, added
another ten.   And this sum was not only sufficient
for his board and lodging, but even for such luxuries as an overcoat lined with Polish beaver, gloves,
scent, and photographs (he often had photographs
taken of himself and used to distribute them among
his friends).   He was neat and demure, slightly
bald, with golden side-whiskers, and he had the
air of a man nearly always ready to oblige.   He
was always busy looking after other people's affairs.
At one time he would be rushing about with a subscription list; at another time he would be freezing
in the early morning at a ticket office to buy tick-
ets for ladies of his acquaintance, or at somebody's
request would be ordering a wreath or a bouquet.
People simply said of him: " Kish will go, Kish
will do it, Kish will buy it."   He was usually un-
successful in carrying out his commissions.   Reproaches were showered upon him, people frequently
forgot to pay him for the things he bought, but he
simply sighed in hard cases and never protested.
He was never particularly delighted nor disappointed; his stories were always long and boring; and
his jokes invariably provoked laughter just because

they were not funny. Thus, one day, for instance, intending to make a joke, he said to Pyotr: " Pyotr, you're not a sturgeon; " and this aroused a general laugh, and he, too, laughed for a long time, much pleased at having made such a successful jest. Whenever one of the professors was buried, he walked in front with the mutes.

Yartsev and Kish usually came in the evening to tea. If the Laptevs were not going to the theatre or a concert, the evening tea lingered on till supper. One evening in February the following conversation took place:

" A work of art is only significant and valuable when there are some serious social problems contained in its central idea," said Kostya, looking wrathfully at Yartsev. " If there is in the work a protest against serfdom, or the author takes up arms against the vulgarity of aristocratic society, the work is significant and valuable. The novels that are taken up with ' Ach! ' and ' Och! ' and ' she loved him, while he ceased to love her,' I tell you, are worthless, and damn them all, I say! "

" I agree with you, Konstantin Ivanovitch," said Yulia Sergeyevna. " One describes a love scene; another, a betrayal; and the third, meeting again after separation. Are there no other subjects? Why, there are many people sick, unhappy, harassed by poverty, to whom reading all that must be distasteful."

It was disagreeable to Laptev to hear his wife, not yet twenty-two, speaking so seriously and coldly about love. He understood why this was so.

" If poetry does not solve questions that seem so important," said Yartsev, " you should turn to works on technical subjects, criminal law, or finance, read scientific pamphlets. What need is there to discuss in ' Romeo and Juliet,' liberty of speech, or the disinfecting of prisons, instead of love, when you can find all that in special articles and textbooks? "

" That's pushing it to the extreme," Kostya interrupted. " We are not talking of giants like Shakespeare or Goethe; we are talking of the hundreds of talented mediocre writers, who would be infinitely more valuable if they would let love alone, and would employ themselves in spreading knowledge and humane ideas among the masses."

Kish, lisping and speaking a little through his nose, began telling the story of a novel he had lately been reading. He spoke circumstantially and without haste. Three minutes passed, then five, then ten, and no one could make out what he was talking about, and his face grew more and more indifferent, and his eyes more and more blank.

" Kish, do be quick over it," Yulia Sergeyevna could not resist saying; " it's really agonizing! "

" Shut up, Kish! " Kostya shouted to him.

They all laughed, and Kish with them.

Fyodor came in. Flushing red in patches, he

greeted them all in a nervous flurry, and led his
brother away into the study. Of late he had taken
to avoiding the company of more than one person
at once.

"Let the young people laugh, while we speak
from the heart in here," he said, settling himself in
a deep arm-chair at a distance from the lamp. "It's
a long time, my dear brother, since we've seen each
other. How long is it since you were at the warehouse? I think it must be a week."

"Yes, there's nothing for me to do there. And
I must confess that the old man wearies me."

"Of course, they could get on at the warehouse
without you and me, but one must have some occupation. 'In the sweat of thy brow thou shalt
eat bread,' as it is written. God loves work."

Pyotr brought in a glass of tea on a tray. Fyodor
drank it without sugar, and asked for more. He
drank a great deal of tea, and could get through as
many as ten glasses in the evening.

"I tell you what, brother," he said, getting up
and going to his brother. "Laying aside philo-
sophic subtleties, you must get elected on to the
town council, and little by little we will get you on
to the local Board, and then to be an alderman.
And as time goes on — you are a clever man and
well-educated — you will be noticed in Petersburg
and asked to go there — active men on the provincial assemblies and town councils are all the fashion

there now — and before you are fifty you'll be a
privy councillor, and have a ribbon across your shoulders."

Laptev made no answer; he knew that all this —
being a privy councillor and having a ribbon over
his shoulder — was what Fyodor desired for himself, and he did not know what to say.

The brothers sat still and said nothing. Fyodor
opened his watch and for a long, long time gazed
into it with strained attention, as though he wanted
to detect the motion of the hand, and the expression of his face struck Laptev as strange.

They were summoned to supper. Laptev went
into the dining-room, while Fyodor remained in the
study. The argument was over and Yartsev was
speaking in the tones of a professor giving a lecture:

"Owing to differences of climate, of energy, of
tastes, of age, equality among men is physically
impossible. But civilised man can make this in-
equality innocuous, as he has already done with
bogs and bears. A learned man succeeded in making a cat, a mouse, a falcon, a sparrow, all eat out
of one plate; and education, one must hope, will do
the same thing with men. Life continually pro-
gresses, civilisation makes enormous advances before our eyes, and obviously a time will come when
we shall think, for instance, the present condition
of the factory population as absurd as we now do

the state of serfdom, in which girls were exchanged
for dogs."

"That won't be for a long while, a very long
while," said Kostya, with a laugh, " not till Roths-
child thinks his cellars full of gold absurd, and till
then the workers may bend their backs and die of
hunger. No; that's not it. We mustn't wait for
it; we must struggle for it. Do you suppose because
the cat eats out of the same saucer as the mouse —
do you suppose that she is influenced by a sense of
conscious intelligence? Not a bit of it! She's made
to do it by force."

" Fyodor and I are rich; our father's a capitalist,
a millionaire. You will have to struggle with us,"
said Laptev, rubbing his forehead with his hand.
" Struggle with me is an idea I cannot grasp. I am
rich, but what has money given me so far? What
has this power given me? In what way am I happier than you? My childhood was slavery, and
money did not save me from the birch. When Nina
was ill and died, my money did not help her. If
people don't care for me, I can't make them like me
if I spend a hundred million."

" But you can do a great deal of good," said
Kish.

" Good, indeed! You spoke to me yesterday of
a mathematical man who is looking for a job. Believe me, I can do as little for him as you can. I
can give money, but that's not what he wants. I

asked a well-known musician to help a poor violin-
ist, and this is what he answered: 'You apply to
me just because you are not a musician yourself.'
In the same way I say to you that you apply for
help to me so confidently because you've never been
in the position of a rich man."

"Why you bring in the comparison with a well-
known musician I don't understand!" said Yulia
Sergeyevna, and she flushed crimson.   "What has
the well-known musician to do with it!"

Her face was quivering with hatred, and she
dropped her eyes to conceal the feeling.   And not
only her husband, but all the men sitting at the table,
knew what the look in her face meant.

"What has the well-known musician got to do
with it?" she said slowly.   "Why, nothing's easier
than helping some one poor."

Silence followed.   Pyotr handed the woodcock,
but they all refused it, and ate nothing but salad.
Laptev did not remember what he had said, but
it was clear to him that it was not his words that
were hateful, but the fact of his meddling in the
conversation at all.

After supper he went into his study; intently,
with a beating heart, expecting further humiliation,
he listened to what was going on in the hall.   An
argument had sprung up there again.   Then Yartsev sat down to the piano and played a sentimental
song.   He was a man of varied accomplishments;

he could play and sing, and even perform conjuring tricks.

"You may please yourselves, my friends, but I'm not going to stay at home," said Yulia. "We must go somewhere."

They decided to drive out of town, and sent Kish to the merchant's club to order a three-horse sledge. They did not ask Laptev to go with them because he did not usually join these expeditions, and because his brother was sitting with him; but he took it to mean that his society bored them, and that he was not wanted in their light-hearted youthful company. And his vexation, his bitter feeling, was so intense that he almost shed tears. He was positively glad that he was treated so ungraciously, that he was scorned, that he was a stupid, dull husband, a money-bag; and it seemed to him, that he would have been even more glad if his wife were to deceive him that night with his best friend, and were afterwards to acknowledge it, looking at him with hatred. . . . He was jealous on her account of their student friends, of actors, of singers, of Yartsev, even of casual acquaintances; and now he had a passionate longing for her really to be unfaithful to him. He longed to find her in another man's arms, and to be rid of this nightmare forever. Fyodor was drinking tea, gulping it noisily. But he, too, got up to go.

"Our old father must have got cataract," he said,

as he put on his fur coat. "His sight has become very poor."

Laptev put on his coat, too, and went out. After seeing his brother part of the way home, he took a sledge and drove to Yar's.

"And this is family happiness!" he said, jeering at himself. "This is love!"

His teeth were chattering, and he did not know if it were jealousy or something else. He walked about near the tables; listened to a comic singer in the hall. He had not a single phrase ready if he should meet his own party; and he felt sure beforehand that if he met his wife, he would only smile pitifully and not cleverly, and that every one would understand what feeling had induced him to come here. He was bewildered by the electric light, the loud music, the smell of powder, and the fact that the ladies he met looked at him. He stood at the doors trying to see and to hear what was going on in the private rooms, and it seemed to him that he was somehow playing a mean, contemptible part on a level with the comic singers and those ladies. Then he went to Strelna, but he found none of his circle there, either; and only when on the way home he was again driving up to Yar's, a three-horse sledge noisily overtook him. The driver was drunk and shouting, and he could hear Yartsev laughing: "Ha, ha, ha!"

Laptev returned home between three and four. Yulia Sergeyevna was in bed. Noticing that she was not asleep, he went up to her and said sharply:

" I understand your repulsion, your hatred, but you might spare me before other people; you might conceal your feelings."

She got up and sat on the bed with her legs dangling. Her eyes looked big and black in the lamplight.

" I beg your pardon," she said.

He could not utter a single word from excitement and the trembling of his whole body; he stood facing her and was dumb. She trembled, too, and sat with the air of a criminal waiting for explanations.

" How I suffer! " he said at last, and he clutched his head. " I'm in hell, and I'm out of my mind."

" And do you suppose it's easy for me? " she asked, with a quiver in her voice. " God alone knows what I go through."

" You've been my wife for six months, but you haven't a spark of love for me in your heart. There's no hope, not one ray of light! Why did you marry me? " Laptev went on with despair. " Why? What demon thrust you into my arms? What did you hope for? What did you want? "

She looked at him with terror, as though she were afraid he would kill her.

" Did I attract you? Did you like me? " he went on, gasping for breath. " No. Then what? What? Tell me what? " he cried. " Oh, the cursed money! The cursed money! "

" I swear to God, no! " she cried, and she crossed

herself.   She seemed to shrink under the insult, and
for the first time he heard her crying.   " I swear
to God, no! " she repeated.   " I didn't think about
your money; I didn't want it.   I simply thought I
should do wrong if I refused you.   I was afraid of
spoiling your life and mine.   And now I am suffering for my mistake.   I'm suffering unbearably! "

She sobbed bitterly, and he saw that she was hurt;
and not knowing what to say, dropped down on the
carpet before her.

" That's enough; that's enough," he muttered.
" I insulted you because I love you madly."   He
suddenly kissed her foot and passionately hugged
it.   " If only a spark of love," he muttered.
" Come, lie to me; tell me a lie!   Don't say it's a
mistake! . . ."

But she went on crying, and he felt that she was
only enduring his caresses as an inevitable consequence of her mistake.   And the foot he had kissed
she drew under her like a bird.   He felt sorry
for her.

She got into bed and covered her head over; he
undressed and got into bed, too.   In the morning
they both felt confused and did not know what to
talk about, and he even fancied she walked unstead-
ily on the foot he had kissed.

Before dinner Panaurov came to say good-bye.
Yulia had an irresistible desire to go to her own
home; it would be nice, she thought, to go away and
have a rest from married life, from the embarrass-

ment and the continual consciousness that she had done wrong. It was decided at dinner that she should set off with Panaurov, and stay with her father for two or three weeks until she was tired of it.

XI

She travelled with Panaurov in a reserved compartment; he had on his head an astrachan cap of peculiar shape.

"Yes, Petersburg did not satisfy me," he said, drawling, with a sigh. "They promise much, but nothing definite. Yes, my dear girl. I have been a Justice of the Peace, a member of the local Board, chairman of the Board of Magistrates, and finally councillor of the provincial administration. I think I have served my country and have earned the right to receive attention; but — would you believe it? — I can never succeed in wringing from the authorities a post in another town. . . ."

Panaurov closed his eyes and shook his head.

"They don't recognise me," he went on, as though dropping asleep. "Of course I'm not an administrator of genius, but, on the other hand, I'm a decent, honest man, and nowadays even that's something rare. I regret to say I have not been always quite straightforward with women, but in my relations with the Russian government I've always been a gentleman. But enough of that," he said, opening his eyes; "let us talk of you. What put it into your head to visit your papa so suddenly?"

" Well. . . . I had a little misunderstanding with my husband," said Yulia, looking at his cap.

" Yes.   What a queer fellow he is!   All the Laptevs are queer.   Your husband's all right — he's nothing out of the way, but his brother Fyodor is a perfect fool."

Panaurov sighed and asked seriously:

" And have you a lover yet? "

Yulia looked at him in amazement and laughed.

" Goodness knows what you're talking about."

It was past ten o'clock when they got out at a big station and had supper.   When the train went on again Panaurov took off his greatcoat and his cap, and sat down beside Yulia.

" You are very charming, I must tell you," he began.   " Excuse me for the eating-house comparison, but you remind me of fresh salted cucumber; it still smells of the hotbed, so to speak, and yet has a smack of the salt and a scent of fennel about it.   As time goes on you will make a magnificent woman, a wonderful, exquisite woman.   If this trip of ours had happened five years ago," he sighed, " I should have felt it my duty to join the ranks of your adorers, but now, alas, I'm a veteran on the retired list."

He smiled mournfully, but at the same time graciously, and put his arm round her waist.

" You must be mad! " she said; she flushed crimson and was so frightened that her hands and feet turned cold.

"Leave off, Grigory Nikolaevitch!"

"What are you afraid of, dear?" he asked softly. "What is there dreadful about it? It's simply that you're not used to it."

If a woman protested he always interpreted it as a sign that he had made an impression on her and attracted her. Holding Yulia round the waist, he kissed her firmly on the cheek, then on the lips, in the full conviction that he was giving her intense gratification. Yulia recovered from her alarm and confusion, and began laughing. He kissed her once more and said, as he put on his ridiculous cap:

"That is all that the old veteran can give you. A Turkish Pasha, a kind-hearted old fellow, was presented by some one — or inherited, I fancy it was — a whole harem. When his beautiful young wives drew up in a row before him, he walked round them, kissed each one of them, and said: 'That is all that I am equal to giving you.' And that's just what I say, too."

All this struck her as stupid and extraordinary, and amused her. She felt mischievous. Standing up on the seat and humming, she got a box of sweets from the shelf, and throwing him a piece of chocolate, shouted:

"Catch!"

He caught it. With a loud laugh she threw him another sweet, then a third, and he kept catching them and putting them into his mouth, looking at her with imploring eyes; and it seemed to her that in his face, his features, his expression, there was a great deal that was feminine and childlike. And when, out of breath, she sat down on the seat and looked at him, laughing, he tapped her cheek with two fingers, and said as though he were vexed:

" Naughty girl! "

" Take it," she said, giving him the box. " I don't care for sweet things."

He ate up the sweets — every one of them, and locked the empty box in his trunk; he liked boxes with pictures on them.

" That's mischief enough, though," he said. " It's time for the veteran to go bye-bye."

He took out of his hold-all a Bokhara dressing-gown and a pillow, lay down, and covered himself with the dressing-gown.

" Good-night, darling! " he said softly, and sighed as though his whole body ached.

And soon a snore was heard. Without the slightest feeling of constraint, she, too, lay down and went to sleep.

When next morning she drove through her native town from the station homewards, the streets seemed to her empty and deserted. The snow looked grey, and the houses small, as though some one had squashed them. She was met by a funeral procession: the dead body was carried in an open coffin with banners.

" Meeting a funeral, they say, is lucky," she thought.

There were white bills pasted in the windows of the house where Nina Fyodorovna used to live.

With a sinking at her heart she drove into her own courtyard and rang at the door. It was opened by a servant she did not know — a plump, sleepy-looking girl wearing a warm wadded jacket. As she went upstairs Yulia remembered how Laptev had declared his love there, but now the staircase was unscrubbed, covered with foot-marks. Upstairs in the cold passage patients were waiting in their out-door coats. And for some reason her heart beat violently, and she was so excited she could scarcely walk.

The doctor, who had grown even stouter, was sitting with a brick-red face and dishevelled hair, drinking tea. Seeing his daughter, he was greatly delighted, and even lacrymose. She thought that she was the only joy in this old man's life, and much moved, she embraced him warmly, and told him she would stay a long time — till Easter. After taking off her things in her own room, she went back to the dining-room to have tea with him. He was pacing up and down with his hands in his pockets, humming, " Ru — ru — ru "; this meant that he was dissatisfied with something.

" You have a gay time of it in Moscow," he said. " I am very glad for your sake. . . . I'm an old man and I need nothing. I shall soon give up the ghost and set you all free. And the wonder

is that my hide is so tough, that I'm alive still!
It's amazing!"

He said that he was a tough old ass that every
one rode on.   They had thrust on him the care of
Nina Fyodorovna, the worry of her children, and
of her burial; and that coxcomb Panaurov would
not trouble himself about it, and had even borrowed
a hundred roubles from him and had never paid
it back.

"Take me to Moscow and put me in a madhouse," said the doctor.   "I'm mad; I'm a simple child, as I still put faith in truth and justice."

Then he found fault with her husband for his
short-sightedness in not buying houses that were
being sold so cheaply.   And now it seemed to Yulia
that she was not the one joy in this old man's life.
While he was seeing his patients, and afterwards
going his rounds, she walked through all the rooms,
not knowing what to do or what to think about.
She had already grown strange to her own town and
her own home.   She felt no inclination to go into
the streets or see her friends; and at the thought
of her old friends and her life as a girl, she felt no
sadness nor regret for the past.

In the evening she dressed a little more smartly
and went to the evening service.   But there were
only poor people in the church, and her splendid
fur coat and hat made no impression.   And it seemed
to her that there was some change in the church as
well as in herself.   In old days she had loved it

when they read the prayers for the day at evening service, and the choir sang anthems such as " I will open my lips." She liked moving slowly in the crowd to the priest who stood in the middle of the church, and then to feel the holy oil on her forehead; now she only waited for the service to be over. And now, going out of the church, she was only afraid that beggars would ask for alms; it was such a bore to have to stop and feel for her pockets; besides, she had no coppers in her pocket now — nothing but roubles.

She went to bed early, and was a long time in going to sleep. She kept dreaming of portraits of some sort, and of the funeral procession she had met that morning. The open coffin with the dead body was carried into the yard, and brought to a standstill at the door; then the coffin was swung backwards and forwards on a sheet, and dashed violently against the door. Yulia woke and jumped up in alarm. There really was a bang at the door, and the wire of the bell rustled against the wall, though no ring was to be heard.

The doctor coughed. Then she heard the servant go downstairs, and then come back.

" Madam! " she said, and knocked at the door. " Madam! "

" What is it? " said Yulia.

" A telegram for you! "

Yulia went out to her with a candle. Behind the servant stood the doctor, in his night-clothes and greatcoat, and he, too, had a candle in his hand.

" Our bell is broken," he said, yawning sleepily. " It ought to have been mended long ago."

Yulia broke open the telegram and read:

" We drink to your health.—YARTSEV, KOTCHE-VOY."

" Ah, what idiots! " she said, and burst out laughing; and her heart felt light and gay.

Going back into her room, she quietly washed and dressed, then she spent a long time in packing her things, until it was daylight, and at midday she set off for Moscow.

XII

In Holy Week the Laptevs went to an exhibition of pictures in the school of painting. The whole family went together in the Moscow fashion, the little girls, the governess, Kostya, and all.

Laptev knew the names of all the well-known painters, and never missed an exhibition. He used sometimes to paint little landscape paintings when he was in the country in the summer, and he fancied he had a good deal of taste, and that if he had studied he might have made a good painter. When he was abroad he sometimes used to go to curio shops, examining the antiques with the air of a connoisseur and giving his opinion on them. When he bought any article he gave just what the shopkeeper liked to ask for it and his purchase remained afterwards in a box in the coach-house till it disappeared altogether. Or going into a print shop, he would slowly and attentively examine the engravings and the bronzes, making various remarks on them, and would buy a common frame or a box of wretched prints. At home he had pictures always of large dimensions but of inferior quality; the best among them were badly hung. It had happened to him more than once to pay large sums for things which had afterwards turned out to be forgeries of the grossest kind. And it was remarkable that, though as a rule timid in the affairs of life, he was exceedingly bold and self-confident at a picture exhibition. Why?

Yulia Sergeyevna looked at the pictures as her husband did, through her open fist or an opera-glass, and was surprised that the people in the pictures were like live people, and the trees like real trees. But she did not understand art, and it seemed to her that many pictures in the exhibition were alike, and she imagined that the whole object in painting was that the figures and objects should stand out as though they were real, when you looked at the picture through your open fist.

" That forest is Shiskin's," her husband explained to her. " He always paints the same thing. . . . But notice snow's never such a lilac colour as that. . . . And that boy's left arm is shorter than his right."

When they were all tired and Laptev had gone

to look for Kostya, that they might go home, Yulia
stopped indifferently before a small landscape.   In
the foreground was a stream, over it a little wooden
bridge; on the further side a path that disappeared
in the dark grass; a field on the right; a copse;
near it a camp fire — no doubt of watchers by night;
and in the distance there was a glow of the evening
sunset.

Yulia imagined walking herself along the little
bridge, and then along the little path further and
further, while all round was stillness, the drowsy
landrails calling and the fire flickering in the distance.   And for some reason she suddenly began
to feel that she had seen those very clouds that
stretched across the red part of the sky, and that
copse, and that field before, many times before.
She felt lonely, and longed to walk on and on along
the path; and there, in the glow of sunset was the
calm reflection of something unearthly, eternal.

" How finely that's painted! " she said, surprised
that the picture had suddenly become intelligible to
her.

" Look, Alyosha!   Do you see how peaceful it
is ? "

She began trying to explain why she liked the
landscape so much, but neither Kostya nor her husband understood her.   She kept looking at the picture with a mournful smile, and the fact that the
others saw nothing special in it troubled her.   Then
she began walking through the rooms and looking

at the pictures again. She tried to understand them and no longer thought that a great many of them were alike. When, on returning home, for the first time she looked attentively at the big picture that hung over the piano in the drawing-room, she felt a dislike for it, and said:

" What an idea to have pictures like that! "

And after that the gilt cornices, the Venetian looking-glasses with flowers on them, the pictures of the same sort as the one that hung over the piano, and also her husband's and Kostya's reflections upon art, aroused in her a feeling of dreariness and vexation, even of hatred.

Life went on its ordinary course from day to day with no promise of anything special. The theatrical season was over, the warm days had come. There was a long spell of glorious weather. One morning the Laptevs attended the district court to hear Kostya, who had been appointed by the court to defend some one. They were late in starting, and reached the court after the examination of the witnesses had begun. A soldier in the reserve was accused of theft and housebreaking. There were a great number of witnesses, washerwomen; they all testified that the accused was often in the house of their employer — a woman who kept a laundry. At the Feast of the Exaltation of the Cross he came late in the evening and began asking for money; he wanted a pick-me-up, as he had been drinking, but no one gave him anything. Then he went away, but an hour afterwards he came back, and brought with him some beer and a soft gingerbread cake for the little girl. They drank and sang songs almost till daybreak, and when in the morning they looked about, the lock of the door leading up into the attic was broken, and of the linen three men's shirts, a petticoat, and two sheets were missing. Kostya asked each witness sarcastically whether she had not drunk the beer the accused had brought. Evidently he was insinuating that the washerwomen had stolen the linen themselves. He delivered his speech without the slightest nervousness, looking angrily at the jury.

He explained what robbery with housebreaking meant, and the difference between that and simple theft. He spoke very circumstantially and convincingly, displaying an unusual talent for speaking at length and in a serious tone about what had been know to every one long before. And it was difficult to make out exactly what he was aiming at. From his long speech the foreman of the jury could only have deduced " that it was housebreaking but not robbery, as the washerwomen had sold the linen for drink themselves; or, if there had been robbery, there had not been housebreaking." But obviously, he said just what was wanted, as his speech moved the jury and the audience, and was very much liked. When they gave a verdict of acquittal, Yulia nodded to Kostya, and afterwards pressed his hand warmly.

In May the Laptevs moved to a country villa at
Sokolniki.   By that time Yulia was expecting a baby.

XIII

More than a year had passed.   Yulia and Yartsev were lying on the grass at Sokolniki not far from
the embankment of the Yaroslav railway; a little
distance away Kotchevoy was lying with hands under his head, looking at the sky.   All three had been
for a walk, and were waiting for the six o'clock train
to pass to go home to tea.

" Mothers see something extraordinary in their
children, that is ordained by nature," said Yulia.
" A mother will stand for hours together by the
baby's cot looking at its little ears and eyes and
nose, and fascinated by them.   If any one else kisses
her baby the poor thing imagines that it gives him
immense pleasure.   And a mother talks of nothing
but her baby.   I know that weakness in mothers,
and I keep watch over myself, but my Olga really
is exceptional.   How she looks at me when I'm
nursing her!   How she laughs!   She's only eight
months old, but, upon my word, I've never seen such
intelligent eyes in a child of three."

" Tell me, by the way," asked Yartsev: " which
do you love most — your husband or your baby? "

Yulia shrugged her shoulders.

" I don't know," she said.   " I never was so very
fond of my husband, and Olga is in reality my first

love. You know that I did not marry Alexey for love. In old days I was foolish and miserable, and thought that I had ruined my life and his, and now I see that love is not necessary — that it is all nonsense."

"But if it is not love, what feeling is it that binds you to your husband? Why do you go on living with him?"

"I don't know. . . . I suppose it must be habit. I respect him, I miss him when he's away for long, but that's — not love. He is a clever, honest man, and that's enough to make me happy. He is very kind and good-hearted. . . ."

"Alyosha's intelligent, Alyosha's good," said Kostya, raising his head lazily; "but, my dear girl, to find out that he is intelligent, good, and interesting, you have to eat a hundredweight of salt with him. . . . And what's the use of his goodness and intelligence? He can fork out money as much as you want, but when character is needed to resist insolence or aggressiveness, he is faint-hearted and overcome with nervousness. People like your amiable Alyosha are splendid people, but they are no use at all for fighting. In fact, they are no use for anything."

At last the train came in sight. Coils of perfectly pink smoke from the funnels floated over the copse, and two windows in the last compartment flashed so brilliantly in the sun, that it hurt their eyes to look at it.

"Tea-time!" said Yulia Sergeyevna, getting up.

She had grown somewhat stouter of late, and her movements were already a little matronly, a little indolent.

"It's bad to be without love though," said Yartsev, walking behind her. "We talk and read of nothing else but love, but we do very little loving ourselves, and that's really bad."

"All that's nonsense, Ivan Gavrilitch," said Yulia. "That's not what gives happiness."

They had tea in the little garden, where mignonette, stocks, and tobacco plants were in flower, and spikes of early gladiolus were just opening. Yartsev and Kotchevoy could see from Yulia's face that she was passing through a happy period of inward peace and serenity, that she wanted nothing but what she had, and they, too, had a feeling of peace and comfort in their hearts. Whatever was said sounded apt and clever; the pines were lovely — the fragrance of them was exquisite as it had never been before; and the cream was very nice; and Sasha was a good, intelligent child.

After tea Yartsev sang songs, accompanying himself on the piano, while Yulia and Kotchevoy sat listening in silence, though Yulia got up from time to time, and went softly indoors, to take a look at the baby and at Lida, who had been in bed for the last two days feverish and eating nothing.

"My friend, my tender friend," sang Yartsev. "No, my friends, I'll be hanged if I understand

why you are all so against love!" he said, flinging
back his head. "If I weren't busy for fifteen hours
of the twenty-four, I should certainly fall in love."

Supper was served on the verandah; it was warm
and still, but Yulia wrapped herself in a shawl and
complained of the damp. When it got dark, she
seemed not quite herself; she kept shivering and begging her visitors to stay a little longer. She regaled them with wine, and after supper ordered
brandy to keep them from going. She didn't want
to be left alone with the children and the servants.

"We summer visitors are getting up a perform-
ance for the children," she said. "We have got
everything — a stage and actors; we are only at a
loss for a play. Two dozen plays of different sorts
have been sent us, but there isn't one that is suitable.
Now, you are fond of the theatre, and are so good
at history," she said, addressing Yartsev. "Write
an historical play for us."

"Well, I might."

The men drank up all the brandy, and prepared
to go.

It was past ten, and for summer-villa people that
was late.

"How dark it is! One can't see a bit," said
Yulia, as she went with them to the gate. "I don't
know how you'll find your way. But, isn't it cold?"

She wrapped herself up more closely and walked
back to the porch.

"I suppose my Alexey's playing cards somewhere," she called to them. "Good-night!"

After the lighted rooms nothing could be seen. Yartsev and Kostya groped their way like blind men to the railway embankment and crossed it.

"One can't see a thing," said Kostya in his bass voice, standing still and gazing at the sky. "And the stars, the stars, they are like new three-pennybits. Gavrilitch!"

"Ah?" Yartsev responded somewhere in the darkness.

"I say, one can't see a thing. Where are you?"

Yartsev went up to him whistling, and took his arm.

"Hi, there, you summer visitors!" Kostya shouted at the top of his voice. "We've caught a socialist."

When he was exhilarated he was always very rowdy, shouting, wrangling with policemen and cabdrivers, singing, and laughing violently.

"Nature be damned," he shouted.

"Come, come," said Yartsev, trying to pacify him. "You mustn't. Please don't."

Soon the friends grew accustomed to the darkness, and were able to distinguish the outlines of the tall pines and telegraph posts. From time to time the sound of whistles reached them from the station and the telegraph wires hummed plaintively. From the copse itself there came no sound, and there was a feeling of pride, strength, and mystery in its silence, and on the right it seemed that the tops of the pines were almost touching the sky. The friends found their path and walked along it. There it was quite dark, and it was only from the long strip of sky dotted with stars, and from the firmly trodden earth under their feet, that they could tell they were walking along a path. They walked along side by side in silence, and it seemed to both of them that people were coming to meet them. Their tipsy exhilaration passed off. The fancy came into Yartsev's mind that perhaps that copse was haunted by the spirits of the Muscovite Tsars, boyars, and patriarchs, and he was on the point of telling Kostya about it, but he checked himself.

When they reached the town gate there was a faint light of dawn in the sky. Still in silence, Yartsev and Kotchevoy walked along the wooden pavement, by the cheap summer cottages, eating-houses, timber-stacks. Under the arch of interlacing branches, the damp air was fragrant of lime-trees, and then a broad, long street opened before them, and on it not a soul, not a light. . . . When they reached the Red Pond, it was daylight.

" Moscow — it's a town that will have to suffer a great deal more," said Yartsev, looking at the Alexyevsky Monastery.

" What put that into your head? "

" I don't know. I love Moscow."

Both Yartsev and Kostya had been born in

Moscow, and adored the town, and felt for some reason antagonistic to every other town. Both were convinced that Moscow was a remarkable town, and Russia a remarkable country. In the Crimea, in the Caucasus, and abroad, they felt dull, uncomfortable, and ill at ease, and they thought their grey Moscow weather very pleasant and healthy. And when the rain lashed at the window-panes and it got dark early, and when the walls of the churches and houses looked a drab, dismal colour, days when one doesn't know what to put on when one is going out — such days excited them agreeably.

At last near the station they took a cab.

"It really would be nice to write an historical play," said Yartsev, "but not about the Lyapunovs or the Godunovs, but of the times of Yaroslav or of Monomach. . . . I hate all historical plays except the monologue of Pimen. When you have to do with some historical authority or even read a text-book of Russian history, you feel that every one in Russia is exceptionally talented, gifted, and interesting; but when I see an historical play at the theatre, Russian life begins to seem stupid, morbid, and not original."

Near Dmitrovka the friends separated, and Yartsev went on to his lodging in Nikitsky Street. He sat half dozing, swaying from side to side, and pondering on the play. He suddenly imagined a terrible din, a clanging noise, and shouts in some unknown language, that might have been Kalmuck, and a village wrapped in flames, and forests near covered with hoarfrost and soft pink in the glow of the fire, visible for miles around, and so clearly that every little fir-tree could be distinguished, and savage men darting about the village on horseback and on foot, and as red as the glow in the sky.

"The Polovtsy," thought Yartsev.

One of them, a terrible old man with a blood-stained face all scorched from the fire, binds to his saddle a young girl with a white Russian face, and the girl looks sorrowful, understanding. . . . Yartsev flung back his head and woke up.

"My friend, my tender friend . . ." he hummed.

As he paid the cabman and went up his stairs, he could not shake off his dreaminess; he saw the flames catching the village, and the forest beginning to crackle and smoke. A huge, wild bear frantic with terror rushed through the village. . . . And the girl tied to the saddle was still looking.

When at last he went into his room it was broad daylight. Two candles were burning by some open music on the piano. On the sofa lay Polina Razsudin wearing a black dress and a sash, with a newspaper in her hand, fast asleep. She must have been playing late, waiting for Yartsev to come home, and, tired of waiting, fell asleep.

"Hullo, she's worn out," he thought.

Carefully taking the newspaper out of her hands, he covered her with a rug. He put out the candles

and went into his bedroom. As he got into bed,
he still thought of his historical play, and the tune
of " My friend, my tender friend " was still ringing in his head. . . .

Two days later Laptev looked in upon him for
a moment to tell him that Lida was ill with diph-
theria, and that Yulia Sergeyevna and her baby had
caught it from her, and five days later came the
news that Lida and Yulia were recovering, but the
baby was dead, and that the Laptevs had left their
villa at Sokolniki and had hastened back to Moscow.

XIV

It had become distasteful to Laptev to be long
at home. His wife was constantly away in the
lodge declaring that she had to look after the little
girls, but he knew that she did not go to the lodge
to give them lessons but to cry in Kostya's room.
The ninth day came, then the twentieth, and then
the fortieth, and still he had to go to the cemetery
to listen to the requiem, and then to wear himself out
for a whole day and night thinking of nothing but
that unhappy baby, and trying to comfort his wife
with all sorts of commonplace expressions. He went
rarely to the warehouse now, and spent most of his
time in charitable work, seizing upon every pretext
requiring his attention, and he was glad when he
had for some trivial reason to be out for the whole
day. He had been intending of late to go abroad,

to study night-refuges, and that idea attracted him now.

It was an autumn day. Yulia had just gone to the lodge to cry, while Laptev lay on a sofa in the study thinking where he could go. Just at that moment Pyotr announced Polina Razsudin. Laptev was delighted; he leapt up and went to meet the unexpected visitor, who had been his closest friend, though he had almost begun to forget her. She had not changed in the least since that evening when he had seen her for the last time, and was just the same as ever.

" Polina," he said, holding out both hands to her. " What ages! If you only knew how glad I am to see you! Do come in! "

Polina greeted him, jerked him by the hand, and without taking off her coat and hat, went into the study and sat down.

" I've come to you for one minute," she said. " I haven't time to talk of any nonsense. Sit down and listen. Whether you are glad to see me or not is absolutely nothing to me, for I don't care a straw for the gracious attentions of you lords of creation. I've only come to you because I've been to five other places already to-day, and everywhere I was met with a refusal, and it's a matter that can't be put off. Listen," she went on, looking into his face. " Five students of my acquaintance, stupid, unintelligent people, but certainly poor, have neglected to pay their fees, and are being excluded from the university. Your wealth makes it your duty to go straight to the university and pay for them."

"With pleasure, Polina."

"Here are their names," she said, giving him a list. "Go this minute; you'll have plenty of time to enjoy your domestic happiness afterwards."

At that moment a rustle was heard through the door that led into the drawing-room; probably the dog was scratching itself. Polina turned crimson and jumped up.

"Your Dulcinea's eavesdropping," she said. "That's horrid!"

Laptev was offended at this insult to Yulia.

"She's not here; she's in the lodge," he said. "And don't speak of her like that. Our child is dead, and she is in great distress."

"You can console her," Polina scoffed, sitting down again; "she'll have another dozen. You don't need much sense to bring children into the world."

Laptev remembered that he had heard this, or something very like it, many times in old days, and it brought back a whiff of the romance of the past, of solitary freedom, of his bachelor life, when he was young and thought he could do anything he chose, when he had neither love for his wife nor memory of his baby.

"Let us go together," he said, stretching.

When they reached the university Polina waited at the gate, while Laptev went into the office; he came back soon afterwards and handed Polina five receipts.

"Where are you going now?" he asked.

"To Yartsev's."

"I'll come with you."

"But you'll prevent him from writing."

"No, I assure you I won't," he said, and looked at her imploringly.

She had on a black hat trimmed with crape, as though she were in mourning, and a short, shabby coat, the pockets of which stuck out. Her nose looked longer than it used to be, and her face looked bloodless in spite of the cold. Laptev liked walking with her, doing what she told him, and listening to her grumbling. He walked along thinking about her, what inward strength there must be in this woman, since, though she was so ugly, so angular, so restless, though she did not know how to dress, and always had untidy hair, and was always somehow out of harmony, she was yet so fascinating.

They went into Yartsev's flat by the back way through the kitchen, where they were met by the cook, a clean little old woman with grey curls; she was overcome with embarrassment, and with a honeyed smile which made her little face look like a pie, said:

"Please walk in."

Yartsev was not at home. Polina sat down to the piano, and beginning upon a tedious, difficult exercise, told Laptev not to hinder her. And with-

out distracting her attention by conversation, he
sat on one side and began turning over the pages
of a "The Messenger of Europe." After practising for two hours — it was the task she set herself every day — she ate something in the kitchen
and went out to her lessons. Laptev read the con-
tinuation of a story, then sat for a long time without
reading and without being bored, glad to think that
he was too late for dinner at home.

"Ha, ha, ha!" came Yartsev's laugh, and he
walked in with ruddy cheeks, looking strong and
healthy, wearing a new coat with bright buttons.
"Ha, ha, ha!"

The friends dined together. Then Laptev lay on
the sofa while Yartsev sat near and lighted a cigar.
It got dark.

"I must be getting old," said Laptev. "Ever
since my sister Nina died, I've taken to constantly
thinking of death."

They began talking of death, of the immortality
of the soul, of how nice it would be to rise again
and fly off somewhere to Mars, to be always idle
and happy, and, above all, to think in a new special way, not as on earth.

"One doesn't want to die," said Yartsev softly.
"No sort of philosophy can reconcile me to death,
and I look on it simply as annihilation. One wants
to live."

"You love life, Gavrilitch?"

"Yes, I love it."

" Do you know, I can never understand myself about that. I'm always in a gloomy mood or else indifferent. I'm timid, without self-confidence; I have a cowardly conscience; I never can adapt my-self to life, or become its master. Some people talk nonsense or cheat, and even so enjoy life, while I consciously do good, and feel nothing but uneasiness or complete indifference. I explain all that, Ga-vrilitch, by my being a slave, the grandson of a serf. Before we plebeians fight our way into the true path, many of our sort will perish on the way."

" That's all quite right, my dear fellow," said Yartsev, and he sighed. " That only proves once again how rich and varied Russian life is. Ah, how rich it is! Do you know, I feel more convinced every day that we are on the eve of the greatest triumph, and I should like to live to take part in it. Whether you like to believe it or not, to my thinking a remarkable generation is growing up. It gives me great enjoyment to teach the children, especially the girls. They are wonderful children! "

Yartsev went to the piano and struck a chord.

" I'm a chemist, I think in chemical terms, and I shall die a chemist," he went on. " But I am greedy, and I am afraid of dying unsatisfied; and chemistry is not enough for me, and I seize upon Russian history, history of art, the science of teach-ing music. . . . Your wife asked me in the sum-mer to write an historical play, and now I'm long-ing to write and write. I feel as though I could sit for three days and three nights without moving, writing all the time. I am worn out with ideas — my brain's crowded with them, and I feel as though there were a pulse throbbing in my head. I don't in the least want to become anything special, to create something great. I simply want to live, to dream, to hope, to be in the midst of everything. . . . Life is short, my dear fellow, and one must make the most of everything."

After this friendly talk, which was not over till midnight, Laptev took to coming to see Yartsev almost every day. He felt drawn to him. As a rule he came towards evening, lay down on the sofa, and waited patiently for Yartsev to come in, without feeling in the least bored. When Yartsev came back from his work, he had dinner, and sat down to work; but Laptev would ask him a question, a conversation would spring up, and there was no more thought of work and at midnight the friends parted very well pleased with one another.

But this did not last long. Arriving one day at Yartsev's, Laptev found no one there but Polina, who was sitting at the piano practising her exercises. She looked at him with a cold, almost hostile expression, and asked without shaking hands:

" Tell me, please: how much longer is this going on ? "

" This? What? " asked Laptev, not understanding.

" You come here every day and hinder Yartsev

from working.   Yartsev is not a tradesman; he is
a scientific man, and every moment of his life is
precious.   You ought to understand and to have
some little delicacy!"

"If you think that I hinder him," said Laptev,
mildly, disconcerted, "I will give up my visits."

"Quite right, too.   You had better go, or he
may be home in a minute and find you here."

The tone in which this was said, and the indifference in Polina's eyes, completely disconcerted him.
She had absolutely no sort of feeling for him now,
except the desire that he should go as soon as possible — and what a contrast it was to her old love
for him!   He went out without shaking hands with
her, and he fancied she would call out to him, bring
him back, but he heard the scales again, and as he
slowly went down the stairs he realised that he had
become a stranger to her now.

Three days later Yartsev came to spend the evening with him.

"I have news," he said, laughing.   "Polina
Nikolaevna has moved into my rooms altogether."
He was a little confused, and went on in a low
voice: "Well, we are not in love with each other,
of course, but I suppose that . . . that doesn't matter.   I am glad I can give her a refuge and peace
and quiet, and make it possible for her not to work
if she's ill.   She fancies that her coming to live
with me will make things more orderly, and that
under her influence I shall become a great scientist.

That's what she fancies. And let her fancy it. In the South they have a saying: ' Fancy makes the fool a rich man.' Ha, ha, ha ! "

Laptev said nothing. Yartsev walked up and down the study, looking at the pictures he had seen so many times before, and said with a sigh:

" Yes, my dear fellow, I am three years older than you are, and it's too late for me to think of real love, and in reality a woman like Polina Nikolaevna is a godsend to me, and, of course, I shall get on capitally with her till we're both old people; but, goodness knows why, one still regrets something, one still longs for something, and I still feel as though I am lying in the Vale of Daghestan and dreaming of a ball. In short, man's never satisfied with what he has."

He went into the drawing-room and began singing as though nothing had happened, and Laptev sat in his study with his eyes shut, and tried to understand why Polina had gone to live with Yartsev. And then he felt sad that there were no lasting, permanent attachments. And he felt vexed that Polina Nikolaevna had gone to live with Yartsev, and vexed with himself that his feeling for his wife was not what it had been.

XV

Laptev sat reading and swaying to and frc in a rocking-chair; Yulia was in the study, and she, too, was reading. It seemed there was nothing to talk about; they had both been silent all day. From time to time he looked at her from over his book and thought: "Whether one marries from passionate love, or without love at all, doesn't it come to the same thing?" And the time when he used to be jealous, troubled, distressed, seemed to him far away. He had succeeded in going abroad, and now he was resting after the journey and looking forward to another visit in the spring to England, which he had very much liked.

And Yulia Sergeyevna had grown used to her sorrow, and had left off going to the lodge to cry. That winter she had given up driving out shopping, had given up the theatres and concerts, and had stayed at home. She never cared for big rooms, and always sat in her husband's study or in her own room, where she had shrines of ikons that had come to her on her marriage, and where there hung on the wall the landscape that had pleased her so much at the exhibition. She spent hardly any money on herself, and was almost as frugal now as she had been in her father's house.

The winter passed cheerlessly. Card-playing was the rule everywhere in Moscow, and if any other recreation was attempted, such as singing, reading, drawing, the result was even more tedious. And since there were few talented people in Moscow, and the same singers and reciters performed at every entertainment, even the enjoyment of art gradually palled and became for many people a tiresome and monotonous social duty.

Moreover, the Laptevs never had a day without something vexatious happening. Old Laptev's eyesight was failing; he no longer went to the warehouse, and the oculist told them that he would soon be blind. Fyodor had for some reason given up going to the warehouse and spent his time sitting at home writing something. Panaurov had got a post in another town, and had been promoted an actual civil councillor, and was now staying at the Dresden. He came to the Laptevs' almost every day to ask for money. Kish had finished his studies at last, and while waiting for Laptev to find him a job, used to spend whole days at a time with them, telling them long, tedious stories. All this was irritating and exhausting, and made daily life unpleasant.

Pyotr came into the study, and announced an unknown lady. On the card he brought in was the name " Josephina Iosefovna Milan."

Yulia Sergeyevna got up languidly and went out limping slightly, as her foot had gone to sleep. In the doorway appeared a pale, thin lady with dark eyebrows, dressed altogether in black. She clasped her hands on her bosom and said supplicatingly:

" M. Laptev, save my children! "

The jingle of her bracelets sounded familiar to him, and he knew the face with patches of powder on it; he recognised her as the lady with whom he had once so inappropriately dined before his marriage.   It was Panaurov's second wife.

"Save my children," she repeated, and her face suddenly quivered and looked old and pitiful. "You alone can save us, and I have spent my last penny coming to Moscow to see you!   My children are starving!"

She made a motion as though she were going to fall on her knees.   Laptev was alarmed, and clutched her by the arm.

"Sit down, sit down . . ." he muttered, making her sit down.   "I beg you to be seated."

"We have no money to buy bread," she said. "Grigory Nikolaevitch is going away to a new post, but he will not take the children and me with him, and the money which you so generously send us he spends only on himself.   What are we to do? What?   My poor, unhappy children!"

"Calm yourself, I beg.   I will give orders that that money shall be made payable to you."

She began sobbing, and then grew calmer, and he noticed that the tears had made little pathways through the powder on her cheeks, and that she was growing a moustache.

"You are infinitely generous, M. Laptev.   But be our guardian angel, our good fairy, persuade Grigory Nikolaevitch not to abandon me, but to take me with him.   You know I love him — I love him insanely; he's the comfort of my life."

Laptev gave her a hundred roubles, and promised to talk to Panaurov, and saw her out to the hall in trepidation the whole time, for fear she should break into sobs or fall on her knees.

After her, Kish made his appearance. Then Kostya came in with his photographic apparatus. Of late he had been attracted by photography and took photographs of every one in the house several times a day. This new pursuit caused him many disappointments, and he had actually grown thinner.

Before evening tea Fyodor arrived. Sitting in a corner in the study, he opened a book and stared for a long time at a page, obviously not reading. Then he spent a long time drinking tea; his face turned red. In his presence Laptev felt a load on his heart; even his silence was irksome to him.

" Russia may be congratulated on the appearance of a new author," said Fyodor. " Joking apart, though, brother, I have turned out a little article — the firstfruits of my pen, so to say — and I've brought it to show you. Read it, dear boy, and tell me your opinion — but sincerely."

He took a manuscript out of his pocket and gave it to his brother. The article was called " The Russian Soul "; it was written tediously, in the colourless style in which people with no talent, but full of secret vanity, usually write. The leading idea of it was that the intellectual man has the right to disbelieve in the supernatural, but it is his duty to conceal his lack of faith, that he may not be a stum-

bling-block and shake the faith of others. Without
faith there is no idealism, and idealism is destined
to save Europe and guide humanity into the true
path.

"But you don't say what Europe has to be saved
from," said Laptev.

"That's intelligible of itself."

"Nothing is intelligible," said Laptev, and he
walked about the room in agitation. "It's not intelligible to me why you wrote it. But that's your
business."

"I want to publish it in pamphlet form."

"That's your affair."

They were silent for a minute. Fyodor sighed
and said:

"It's an immense regret to me, dear brother,
that we think differently. Oh, Alyosha, Alyosha,
my darling brother! You and I are true Russians,
true believers, men of broad nature; all of these
German and Jewish crochets are not for us. You
and I are not wretched upstarts, you know, but rep-
resentatives of a distinguished merchant family."

"What do you mean by a distinguished family?"
said Laptev, restraining his irritation. "A distinguished family! The landowners beat our grandfather and every low little government clerk punched
him in the face. Our grandfather thrashed our
father, and our father thrashed us. What has your
distinguished family done for us? What sort of
nerves, what sort of blood, have we inherited? For

nearly three years you've been arguing like an ignorant deacon, and talking all sorts of nonsense, and now you've written — this slavish drivel here! While I, while I! Look at me. . . . No elasticity, no boldness, no strength of will; I tremble over every step I take as though I should be flogged for it. I am timid before nonentities, idiots, brutes, who are immeasurably my inferiors mentally and morally; I am afraid of porters, doorkeepers, policemen, gendarmes. I am afraid of every one, because I was born of a mother who was terrified, and because from a child I was beaten and frightened! . . . You and I will do well to have no children. Oh, God, grant that this distinguished merchant family may die with us!"

Yulia Sergeyevna came into the study and sat down at the table.

"Are you arguing about something here?" she asked. "Am I interrupting?"

"No, little sister," answered Fyodor. "Our discussion was of principles. Here, you are abusing the family," he added, turning to his brother. "That family has created a business worth a million, though. That stands for something, anyway!"

"A great distinction — a business worth a million! A man with no particular brains, without abilities, by chance becomes a trader, and then when he has grown rich he goes on trading from day to day, with no sort of system, with no aim, without having any particular greed for money. He trades mechanically, and money comes to him of itself, without his going to meet it. He sits all his life at his work, likes it only because he can domineer over his clerks and get the better of his customers. He's a churchwarden because he can domineer over the choristers and keep them under his thumb; he's the patron of a school because he likes to feel the teacher is his subordinate and enjoys lording it over him. The merchant does not love trading, he loves domi- nating, and your warehouse is not so much a com- mercial establishment as a torture chamber!   And for a business like yours, you want clerks who have been deprived of individual character and personal life — and you make them such by forcing them in childhood to lick the dust for a crust of bread, and you've trained them from childhood to believe that you are their benefactors. No fear of your taking a university man into your warehouse ! "

"University men are not suitable for our busi- ness."

"That's not true," cried Laptev.   "It's a lie ! "

"Excuse me, it seems to me you spit into the well from which you drink yourself," said Fyodor, and he got up. "Our business is hateful to you, yet you make use of the income from it."

"Aha! We've spoken our minds," said Laptev, and he laughed, looking angrily at his brother. "Yes, if I didn't belong to your distinguished fam- ily — if I had an ounce of will and courage, I should

long ago have flung away that income, and have
gone to work for my living. But in your warehouse
you've destroyed all character in me from a child!
I'm your product."

Fyodor looked at the clock and began hurriedly
saying good-bye. He kissed Yulia's hand and went
out, but instead of going into the hall, walked into
the drawing-room, then into the bedroom.

"I've forgotten how the rooms go," he said in
extreme confusion. "It's a strange house. Isn't
it a strange house!"

He seemed utterly overcome as he put on his coat,
and there was a look of pain on his face. Laptev
felt no more anger; he was frightened, and at the
same time felt sorry for Fyodor, and the warm,
true love for his brother, which seemed to have died
down in his heart during those three years, awoke,
and he felt an intense desire to express that love.

"Come to dinner with us to-morrow, Fyodor,"
he said, and stroked him on the shoulder. "Will
you come?"

"Yes, yes; but give me some water."

Laptev ran himself to the dining-room to take the
first thing he could get from the sideboard. This
was a tall beer-jug. He poured water into it and
brought it to his brother. Fyodor began drinking,
but bit a piece out of the jug; they heard a crunch,
and then sobs. The water ran over his fur coat
and his jacket, and Laptev, who had never seen men
cry, stood in confusion and dismay, not knowing

what to do. He looked on helplessly while Yulia
and the servant took off Fyodor's coat and helped
him back again into the room, and went with him,
feeling guilty.

Yulia made Fyodor lie down on the sofa and
knelt beside him.

" It's nothing," she said, trying to comfort him.
" It's your nerves. . . ."

" I'm so miserable, my dear! " he said. " I am
so unhappy, unhappy . . . but all the time I've
been hiding it, I've been hiding it! "

He put his arm round her neck and whispered
in her ear:

" Every night I see my sister Nina. She comes
and sits in the chair near my bed. . . ."

When, an hour later, he put on his fur coat in
the hall, he was smiling again and ashamed to face
the servant. Laptev went with him to Pyatnitsky
Street.

" Come and have dinner with us to-morrow," he
said on the way, holding him by the arm, " and at
Easter we'll go abroad together. You absolutely
must have a change, or you'll be getting quite morbid."

When he got home Laptev found his wife in a
state of great nervous agitation. The scene with
Fyodor had upset her, and she could not recover her
composure. She wasn't crying but kept tossing on
the bed, clutching with cold fingers at the quilt, at

the pillows, at her husband's hands. Her eyes looked big and frightened.

"Don't go away from me, don't go away," she said to her husband. "Tell me, Alyosha, why have I left off saying my prayers? What has become of my faith? Oh, why did you talk of religion before me? You've shaken my faith, you and your friends. I never pray now."

He put compresses on her forehead, chafed her hands, gave her tea to drink, while she huddled up to him in terror. . . .

Towards morning she was worn out and fell asleep, while Laptev sat beside her and held her hand. So that he could get no sleep. The whole day afterwards he felt shattered and dull, and wandered listlessly about the rooms without a thought in his head.

XVI

The doctor said that Fyodor's mind was affected. Laptev did not know what to do in his father's house, while the dark warehouse in which neither his father nor Fyodor ever appeared now seemed to him like a sepulchre. When his wife told him that he absolutely must go every day to the warehouse and also to his father's, he either said nothing, or began talking irritably of his childhood, saying that it was beyond his power to forgive his father for his past, that the warehouse and the house in Pyatnitsky Street were hateful to him, and so on.

One Sunday morning Yulia went herself to Pyatnitsky Street. She found old Fyodor Stepanovitch in the same big drawing-room in which the service had been held on her first arrival. Wearing slippers, and without a cravat, he was sitting motionless in his arm-chair, blinking with his sightless eyes.

"It's I — your daughter-in-law," she said, going up to him. "I've come to see how you are."

He began breathing heavily with excitement.

Touched by his affliction and his loneliness, she kissed his hand; and he passed his hand over her face and head, and having satisfied himself that it was she, made the sign of the cross over her.

"Thank you, thank you," he said. "You know I've lost my eyes and can see nothing. . . . I can dimly see the window and the fire, but people and things I cannot see at all. Yes, I'm going blind, and Fyodor has fallen ill, and without the master's eye things are in a bad way now. If there is any irregularity there's no one to look into it; and folks soon get spoiled. And why is it Fyodor has fallen ill? Did he catch cold? Here I have never ailed in my life and never taken medicine. I never saw anything of doctors."

And, as he always did, the old man began boasting. Meanwhile the servants hurriedly laid the table and brought in lunch and bottles of wine.

Ten bottles were put on the table; one of them was in the shape of the Eiffel Tower. There was a whole dish of hot pies smelling of jam, rice, and fish.

" I beg my dear guest to have lunch," said the old man.

She took him by the arm, led him to the table, and poured him out a glass of vodka.

" I will come to you again to-morrow," she said, " and I'll bring your granchildren, Sasha and Lida. They will be sorry for you, and fondle you."

" There's no need. Don't bring them. They are illegitimate."

" Why are they illegitimate? Why, their father and mother were married."

" Without my permission. I do not bless them, and I don't want to know them. Let them be."

" You speak strangely, Fyodor Stepanovitch," said Yulia, with a sigh.

" It is written in the Gospel: children must fear and honour their parents."

" Nothing of the sort. The Gospel tells us that we must forgive even our enemies."

" One can't forgive in our business. If you were to forgive every one, you would come to ruin in three years."

" But to forgive, to say a kind, friendly word to any one, even a sinner, is something far above business, far above wealth."

Yulia longed to soften the old man, to awaken a

feeling of compassion in him, to move him to repentance; but he only listened condescendingly to all she said, as a grown-up person listens to a child.

"Fyodor Stepanovitch," said Yulia resolutely, "you are an old man, and God soon will call you to Himself. He won't ask you how you managed your business, and whether you were successful in it, but whether you were gracious to people; or whether you were harsh to those who were weaker than you, such as your servants, your clerks."

"I was always the benefactor of those that served me; they ought to remember me in their prayers forever," said the old man, with conviction, but touched by Yulia's tone of sincerity, and anxious to give her pleasure, he said: "Very well; bring my grandchildren to-morrow. I will tell them to buy me some little presents for them."

The old man was slovenly in his dress, and there was cigar ash on his breast and on his knees; apparently no one cleaned his boots, or brushed his clothes. The rice in the pies was half cooked, the tablecloth smelt of soap, the servants tramped noisily about the room. And the old man and the whole house had a neglected look, and Yulia, who felt this, was ashamed of herself and of her husband.

"I will be sure to come and see you to-morrow," she said.

She walked through the rooms, and gave orders for the old man's bedroom to be set to rights, and the lamp to be lighted under the ikons in it. Fyodor, sitting in his own room, was looking at an open book without reading it. Yulia talked to him and told the servants to tidy his room, too; then she went downstairs to the clerks. In the middle of the room where the clerks used to dine, there was an unpainted wooden post to support the ceiling and to prevent its coming down. The ceilings in the basement were low, the walls covered with cheap paper, and there was a smell of charcoal fumes and cooking. As it was a holiday, all the clerks were at home, sitting on their bedsteads waiting for dinner. When Yulia went in they jumped up, and answered her questions timidly, looking up at her from under their brows like convicts.

"Good heavens! What a horrid room you have!" she said, throwing up her hands. "Aren't you crowded here?"

"Crowded, but not aggrieved," said Makeitchev. "We are greatly indebted to you, and will offer up our prayers for you to our Heavenly Father."

"The congruity of life with the conceit of the personality," said Potchatkin.

And noticing that Yulia did not understand Potchatkin, Makeitchev hastened to explain:

"We are humble people and must live according to our position."

She inspected the boys' quarters, and then the kitchen, made acquaintance with the housekeeper, and was thoroughly dissatisfied.

When she got home she said to her husband:

"We ought to move into your father's house and settle there for good as soon as possible. And you will go every day to the warehouse."

Then they both sat side by side in the study without speaking. His heart was heavy, and he did not want to move into Pyatnitsky Street or to go into the warehouse; but he guessed what his wife was thinking, and could not oppose her. He stroked her cheek and said:

"I feel as though our life is already over, and that a grey half-life is beginning for us. When I knew that my brother Fyodor was hopelessly ill, I shed tears; we spent our childhood and youth together, when I loved him with my whole soul. And now this catastrophe has come, and it seems, too, as though, losing him, I am finally cut away from my past. And when you said just now that we must move into the house in Pyatnitsky Street, to that prison, it began to seem to me that there was no future for me either."

He got up and walked to the window.

"However that may be, one has to give up all thoughts of happiness," he said, looking out into the street. "There is none. I never have had any, and I suppose it doesn't exist at all. I was happy once in my life, though, when I sat at night under your parasol. Do you remember how you left your parasol at Nina's?" he asked, turning to his wife. "I was in love with you then, and I re-

member I spent all night sitting under your parasol,
and was perfectly blissful."

Near the book-case in the study stood a mahogany
chest with bronze fittings where Laptev kept various
useless things, including the parasol. He took it
out and handed it to his wife.

"Here it is."

Yulia looked for a minute at the parasol, recognised it, and smiled mournfully.

"I remember," she said. "When you proposed
to me you held it in your hand." And seeing that
he was preparing to go out, she said: "Please
come back early if you can. I am dull without you."

And then she went into her own room, and gazed
for a long time at the parasol.

XVII

In spite of the complexity of the business and
the immense turnover, there were no bookkeepers
in the warehouse, and it was impossible to make
anything out of the books kept by the cashier in the
office. Every day the warehouse was visited by
agents, German and English, with whom the clerks
talked politics and religion. A man of noble birth,
ruined by drink, an ailing, pitiable creature, used to
come to translate the foreign correspondence in the
office; the clerks used to call him a midge, and put
salt in his tea. And altogether the whole concern
struck Laptev as a very queer business.

He went to the warehouse every day and tried to

establish a new order of things; he forbade them to thrash the boys and to jeer at the buyers, and was violently angry when the clerks gleefully despatched to the provinces worthless shop-soiled goods as though they were new and fashionable. Now he was the chief person in the warehouse, but still, as before, he did not know how large his fortune was, whether his business was doing well, how much the senior clerks were paid, and so on. Potchatkin and Makeitchev looked upon him as young and inexperienced, concealed a great deal from him, and whispered mysteriously every evening with his blind old father.

It somehow happened at the beginning of June that Laptev went into the Bubnovsky restaurant with Potchatkin to talk business with him over lunch. Potchatkin had been with the Laptevs a long while, and had entered their service at eight years old. He seemed to belong to them — they trusted him fully; and when on leaving the warehouse he gathered up all the takings from the till and thrust them into his pocket, it never aroused the slightest suspicion. He was the head man in the business and in the house, and also in the church, where he performed the duties of churchwarden in place of his old master. He was nicknamed Malyuta Skuratov on account of his cruel treatment of the boys and clerks under him.

When they went into the restaurant he nodded to a waiter and said:

" Bring us, my lad, half a bodkin and twenty-four unsavouries."

After a brief pause the waiter brought on a tray half a bottle of vodka and some plates of various kinds of savouries.

" Look here, my good fellow," said Potchatkin. " Give us a plateful of the source of all slander and evil-speaking, with mashed potatoes."

The waiter did not understand; he was puzzled, and would have said something, but Potchatkin looked at him sternly and said:

" Except."

The waiter thought intently, then went to consult with his colleagues, and in the end guessing what was meant, brought a plateful of tongue. When they had drunk a couple of glasses and had had lunch, Laptev asked:

" Tell me, Ivan Vassilitch, is it true that our business has been dropping off for the last year? "

" Not a bit of it."

" Tell me frankly and honestly what income we have been making and are making, and what our profits are. We can't go on in the dark. We had a balancing of the accounts at the warehouse lately, but, excuse me, I don't believe in it; you think fit to conceal something from me and only tell the truth to my father. You have been used to being diplomatic from your childhood, and now you can't get on without it. And what's the use of it? So I beg you to be open. What is our position? "

" It all depends upon the fluctuation of credit,"
Potchatkin answered after a moment's pause.

" What do you understand by the fluctuation of
credit? "

Potchatkin began explaining, but Laptev could
make nothing of it, and sent for Makeitchev. The
latter promptly made his appearance, had some
lunch after saying grace, and in his sedate, mellow
baritone began saying first of all that the clerks were
in duty bound to pray night and day for their benefactors.

" By all means, only allow me not to consider myself your benefactor," said Laptev.

" Every man ought to remember what he is, and
to be conscious of his station.   By the grace of God
you are a father and benefactor to us, and we are
your slaves."

" I am sick of all that ! " said Laptev, getting
angry.   " Please be a benefactor to me now.
Please explain the position of our business.   Give
up looking upon me as a boy, or to-morrow I shall
close the business.   My father is blind, my brother
is in the asylum, my nieces are only children.   I hate
the business; I should be glad to go away, but there's
no one to take my place, as you know.   For goodness' sake, drop your diplomacy ! "

They went to the warehouse to go into the accounts; then they went on with them at home in
the evening, the old father himself assisting. Initi-
ating his son into his commercial secrets, the old

man spoke as though he were engaged, not in trade,
but in sorcery. It appeared that the profits of the
business were increasing approximately ten per cent.
per annum, and that the Laptevs' fortune, reckoning only money and paper securities, amounted to six
million roubles.

When at one o'clock at night, after balancing the
accounts, Laptev went out into the open air, he was
still under the spell of those figures. It was a still,
sultry, moonlight night. The white walls of the
houses beyond the river, the heavy barred gates,
the stillness and the black shadows, combined to give
the impression of a fortress, and nothing was want-
ing to complete the picture but a sentinel with a
gun. Laptev went into the garden and sat down
on a seat near the fence, which divided them from
the neighbour's yard, where there was a garden,
too. The bird-cherry was in bloom. Laptev remembered that the tree had been just as gnarled
and just as big when he was a child, and had not
changed at all since then. Every corner of the garden and of the yard recalled the far-away past.
And in his childhood, too, just as now, the whole
yard bathed in moonlight could be seen through the
sparse trees, the shadows had been mysterious and
forbidding, a black dog had lain in the middle of
the yard, and the clerks' windows had stood wide
open. And all these were cheerless memories.

The other side of the fence, in the neighbour's
yard, there was a sound of light steps.

" My sweet, my precious . . ." said a man's voice so near the fence that Laptev could hear the man's breathing.

Now they were kissing. Laptev was convinced that the millions and the business which was so distasteful to him were ruining his life, and would make him a complete slave. He imagined how, little by little, he would grow accustomed to his position; would, little by little, enter into the part of the head of a great firm; would begin to grow dull and old, die in the end, as the average man usually does die, in a decrepit, soured old age, making every one about him miserable and depressed. But what hindered him from giving up those millions and that business, and leaving that yard and garden which had been hateful to him from his childhood?

The whispering and kisses the other side of the fence disturbed him. He moved into the middle of the yard, and, unbuttoning his shirt over his chest, looked at the moon, and it seemed to him that he would order the gate to be unlocked, and would go out and never come back again. His heart ached sweetly with the foretaste of freedom; he laughed joyously, and pictured how exquisite, poetical, and even holy, life might be. . . .

But he still stood and did not go away, and kept asking himself: " What keeps me here? " And he felt angry with himself and with the black dog, which still lay stretched on the stone yard, instead of running off to the open country, to the woods, where it would have been free and happy. It was clear that that dog and he were prevented from leaving the yard by the same thing; the habit of bondage, of servitude. . . .

At midday next morning he went to see his wife, and that he might not be dull, asked Yartsev to go with him. Yulia Sergeyevna was staying in a summer villa at Butovo, and he had not been to see her for five days. When they reached the station the friends got into a carriage, and all the way there Yartsev was singing and in raptures over the exquisite weather. The villa was in a great park not far from the station. At the beginning of an avenue, about twenty paces from the gates, Yulia Sergeyevna was sitting under a broad, spreading poplar, waiting for her guests. She had on a light, elegant dress of a pale cream colour trimmed with lace, and in her hand she had the old familiar parasol. Yartsev greeted her and went on to the villa from which came the sound of Sasha's and Lida's voices, while Laptev sat down beside her to talk of business matters.

"Why is it you haven't been for so long?" she said, keeping his hand in hers. "I have been sitting here for days watching for you to come. I miss you so when you are away!"

She stood up and passed her hand over his hair, and scanned his face, his shoulders, his hat, with interest.

"You know I love you," she said, and flushed

crimson. " You are precious to me. Here you've come. I see you, and I'm so happy I can't tell you. Well, let us talk. Tell me something."

She had told him she loved him, and he could only feel as though he had been married to her for ten years, and that he was hungry for his lunch. She had put her arm round his neck, tickling his cheek with the silk of her dress; he cautiously removed her hand, stood up, and without uttering a single word, walked to the villa. The little girls ran to meet him.

" How they have grown ! " he thought. " And what changes in these three years. . . . But one may have to live another thirteen years, another thirty years. . . . What is there in store for us in the future? If we live, we shall see."

He embraced Sasha and Lida, who hung upon his neck, and said:

" Grandpapa sends his love. . . . Uncle Fyodor is dying. Uncle Kostya has sent a letter from America and sends you his love in it. He's bored at the exhibition and will soon be back. And Uncle Alyosha is hungry."

Then he sat on the verandah and saw his wife walking slowly along the avenue towards the house. She was deep in thought; there was a mournful, charming expression in her face, and her eyes were bright with tears. She was not now the slender, fragile, pale-faced girl she used to be; she was a mature, beautiful, vigorous woman. And Laptev saw the enthusiasm with which Yartsev looked at her when he met her, and the way her new, lovely expression was reflected in his face, which looked mournful and ecstatic too. One would have thought that he was seeing her for the first time in his life. And while they were at lunch on the verandah, Yartsev smiled with a sort of joyous shyness, and kept gazing at Yulia and at her beautiful neck. Laptev could not help watching them while he thought that he had perhaps another thirteen, another thirty years of life before him. . . . And what would he have to live through in that time? What is in store for us in the future?

And he thought:

"Let us live, and we shall see."

1895